REINVENTING

HOME

REINVENTING

HOME

Six Working Women Look at Their Home Lives

LAURIE ABRAHAM • MARY BETH DANIELSON
NANCY EBERLE • LAURA GREEN
JANICE ROSENBERG • CARROLL STONER

A PLUME BOOK

PLUME
Published by the Penguin Group
Penguin Books USA Inc., 375 Hudson Street, New York, New York 10014, U.S.A.
Penguin Books Ltd, 27 Wrights Lane, London W8 5TZ, England
Penguin Books Australia Ltd, Ringwood, Victoria, Australia
Penguin Books Canada Ltd, 2801 John Street, Markham, Ontario, Canada L3R 1B4
Penguin Books (N.Z.) Ltd, 182-190 Wairau Road, Auckland 10, New Zealand

Penguin Books Ltd, Registered Offices: Harmondsworth, Middlesex, England

First published by Plume, an imprint of New American Library,
a division of Penguin Books USA Inc.

First Printing, March, 1991
10 9 8 7 6 5 4 3

 REGISTERED TRADEMARK—MARCA REGISTRADA

LIBRARY OF CONGRESS CATALOGING IN PUBLICATION DATA:

Reinventing home: six working women look at their home lives / by Laurie
   Abraham, Mary Beth Danielson, Nancy Eberle, Laura Green, Janice Rosenberg,
   Carroll Stoner.
       p.   cm.
   ISBN 0-452-26583-5
   1. Home—United States.   2. Working mothers—United States—Attitudes.
HQ536.A8   1991
306.87—dc20   90-46440
                                                                   CIP

Printed in the United States of America
Set in Janson
Designed by Eve L. Kirch

We were six when this book began, but now we are only five. Nancy Eberle, who lived with a grace, generosity, and insight that the rest of us admired and would have emulated if we could, died in 1988. We dedicate this book to her memory.

From the beginning, this was a project nurtured by women who believed in it. For their commitment, guidance, and support we want to thank our agent, Connie Clausen, and editors, Joyce Engelson and Alexia Dorszynski, along with Toni Rachiele, Melissa Jacoby, Leslie Schneider, Kristin Olson, Maureen Donnelly, and Nancy Dubitsky. To them all, affection and appreciation.

—C.S. & L.G.

CONTENTS

VISIONS OF MASTERY

BOUND FOR HOME

DRAWING THE LINE

FRESH STARTS

A NOTE FROM THE EDITORS

This book is about reinventing the home and reconsidering our lives within it. It is about men and women, possessions and commitments, accumulations and unloading, children and room-mates. It is about the conviction that a rich domestic life is worth having and therefore worth thinking about. The six of us have had more than a hundred years of domestic living under our collective belt and we have some very firm opinions.

One of them is that domestic life is a serious matter. This is not a book about style. We are not exalting the couple who sold their business, moved to the country, and started a flour-ishing trade in dried cranberries while writing books on the home education movement and reorganizing the County Board of Supervisors. It is not about tech, low or high, or arranging flowers, because we are not interior designers. We know that beautiful rooms lift the spirit, but we also know that they do not give a home spiritual sustenance.

This book is not about "new traditionalists," which is just another name for a woman who has chosen to stay home when her children are small. Nor is it about the dirty little moral war between those women and the women who hold jobs.

This book is about the whole messy business of our five-to-nine lives, about living alone for the first time, and about taking pride in doing what we do well, whether it is honing knives surgically sharp or rehabbing a house. It is about little things that make a stolen day at home delicious—sneaking home to play with the children, staying home to linger over a cup of French roast, repotting the plants when we have reports to write. It is about tolerating roommates and learning to ignore house guests. It is also about things that make it hard to go home, about feeling trivial, about boredom, about suddenly single parents who must figure out what home ought to be all over again.

This book is about quandaries—because we simply do not know how big a place our homes should hold in our lives or how to shape old notions to fit the new women we have become. It is about wanting some order without having to hold to unreasonably rigid standards. It is about wanting to live in a welcoming place without having to put a lot of effort into prettifying. It is about the time and energy we put into making dinner or organizing a closet, even if taking pleasure in such things is considered evidence of an inferior intellect.

We wanted to write about our desire to hang on to the traditions we love at a time when we are forced to reinvent our attitudes about everything that happens in our domestic lives, including how much power the home gives us and how much energy it demands. This book is about the ways we make families from disparate friends in our search for peace, place, and belonging. It is about the discoveries we have made about the places underfoot—for what could be closer to home and thus harder for a generation of perpetually farsighted women to see than home itself?

As writers in our twenties, thirties, forties, and fifties, we are united by the conviction that domestic matters are worthy of the reflection characteristic of our craft. We believe that thinking about our home lives is a good thing, that there is a great deal to think about, and that we probably don't think about it enough. We know that buying a bed is not a crucial task and that one can tell family stories without understanding their importance, but we are aware that such domestic bits and pieces add up to a whole that is worth contemplating.

We know that things are not quite right at home. We see women who cling to the domestic standards of their childhoods although they work long hours at their jobs. We see women who have jettisoned domestic life and have failed to replace it with anything else. We see the ambivalence of women who think it is unprofessional to talk about their home lives, although their yearning to do so is palpable.

We know that women—and men, too—need to go home and curl up with a magazine without feeling they should be doing something more important. We realize that for some of us, the only place to find that sense of home is at someone else's place.

We need to stop feeling silly, if not downright embarrassed, about our interest in all these matters. Although women have changed, we still fear that a book about domestic life is suspect, as if home were only housework. The quarter-century since the women's movement began has not been long enough for women to stop being jittery about their status. We are wary of being taken for recidivists, or for women who never woke up. We wrestle with the historic denigration of women's work that plagues us to this day. Perhaps inevitably, the person who made home a work of art was not a woman but a man, Thomas Jefferson, who raised domestic life at Monticello to a state of grace that it rarely achieved elsewhere. We yearn to discuss our gardens with his same dignity and delight.

On the other hand . . .

On the other hand, Monticello exists today not because Jefferson grew French peas in Virginia soil but because of his extraordinary life as a statesman and a leader. As history tells us, there is more to life than the house on the hill. Let us be very clear about that. Jefferson managed and directed; he didn't worry about scrubbing pots or mending britches. If our lives have been weighted toward work recently, it is because we had enough pot scrubbing, enough of just running the house, enough of its foreshortened vistas. We hated the triviality of housekeeping. We will always be weary of looking at the eggy plates in the sink, at the dirt, the lost clothes balled up under the bed. We are frustrated that our houses don't work like work and never will. The crisp regularity of the office is nowhere to be found in the double helix of domestic life.

No, home alone cannot fill our lives. The combination of home and career is what makes life work. We ask, along with millions of other women, not which is better but how to keep the parts in balance. And we want to know how to achieve balance in a world where home means a different thing to each of us, where a chair is one thing to the man who collapses into it at the end of the day and another to the woman who bought it on her lunch hour.

We are tied to our homes by the joys and satisfactions they bring us. And we are bound to them, as obviously as if we were tied to a chair, by guilt and by others' expectations that we will make our homes work for them. Homes are work for women, far more than for men, and so they can limit us by sapping our energy, filling up our precious time, giving us a too-easy definition of who we are.

This book is an invitation, if not a plea, to reconsider domestic life and reinvent the home as a place to nourish the scenes we've so carefully created. We are bound to our domestic lives on emotional, intellectual, and practical levels. If home is part of a complete life and we believe it is, we must find ways to create domestic lives that fit our needs and make ourselves sanctuaries that are deliberate, intimate, and nourishing.

In a new place, we are free to reinvent ourselves, to end the impossible expectation of the past. We believe that new place should be home.

—CARROLL STONER

—LAURA GREEN

MOMENTS
OF GRACE

At Home

NANCY EBERLE

The other day I found out what it's like to feel at home, at home. My epiphany occurred during the course of spring vacation, which my ten-year-old daughter had invited her best friend to spend with us. Our destination was the farm.

The farm is the place my husband and I left the city for seven years ago, and where we spent five joyous and difficult years before deciding to move back. Today I suppose you'd call it our second home, since we use it mostly on weekends and vacations, but it is a designation that hurts. If financial disaster strikes, it is the place we would keep. If civil disaster strikes, it is the place we would struggle toward. With or without disaster, it is the home of our hearts.

It was dark outside when we arrived, and dark within as well: We had turned off the electricity on our last trip out, hoping to stanch the perplexing flow of kilowatts and dollars that continues even in our absence. I was standing at the door to the kitchen when the lights came on, and I thought I had never seen anything so inviting in my life. Through the window over the kitchen sink and across the valley you could see the lights of town twinkling far away. Above the apple-green counter on either side of the sink hung the beautiful brown pottery we'd brought back from Guatemala but never use any more because we'd have to wash off a glaze of grease first. The old pine table (not a real table, but one made from a hollow

7

door in the early, poorer days of our marriage) glowed under the drop lamp that hangs from the raftered ceiling, and the hodgepodge of chairs of different sizes and colors around it didn't matter. The floor was filthy—I noticed that—but it was filthy Mexican quarry tile and therefore not so bad.

Anyone who has taken a long vacation has experienced moments such as this, when the house looks as it must to someone who doesn't live there. You see the baskets hanging from the beams and think how terrific they look, instead of how there aren't enough to make a good showing. You look at the humble-jumble on the freezer—binoculars and bird books and dried mushrooms and coupons and the apples no one will eat and masking tape and telephone books and the mail—and are amused by the idiosyncrasy of the assemblage instead of annoyed that it will all have to be put away. You gaze upon the living room and think how wonderfully homey it looks instead of wishing you hadn't been quite so cavalier about driving in four-inch nails wherever you chose. Like the faces of friends from whom you've been separated (which also become momentarily strange in our absence), it all becomes familiar again. Try as you might, you can no more get back that moment's pure vision and its revelation than you can reclaim your innocence. And in a way, what we are talking about here is innocence: being innocent of the effort and the burden of responsibility involved in such scenes. For that brief instant what we see is just—what we see.

In the spirit of that moment I decided I liked everything exactly the way it was and that I wasn't going to clean house until we got a rainy day, which we surely would in the course of an April week. I said it out loud, for emphasis: "Hey, you guys, we're not going to clean up until it rains," but no one paid any attention. It was the last thing on their minds.

We hadn't been to the farm since Christmas and were looking forward to a week of spring weather in a glorious setting—and that is what we got. Spring in the city is mostly a matter of balmy weather, bicyclists in the park, and buds on the trees; in the country it is an entire landscape awakening. Huge carp as big as a man's arm thrashing and splashing in the pond where they spawn; bluebirds and robins and field sparrows singing their hearts out. The ewes and the lambs baaaing and maaaing and ruaahing as they spread themselves out over the hillside; and the hepatica and Dutchman's britches spreading themselves over the surrounding woods. At least once a day you give thanks that you are alive.

And that, for two days, was what it was like. The sun shone down with an unseasonable warmth. We studied the perennial border each morning for new signs of growth and gazed with delight at the volunteer lettuce and parsley, chives and coriander that had sprung up in our primitive greenhouse during our absence. We policed the grounds with energy. We flew a kite. We hunted for arrowheads in the fields and wild-flowers in the woods. And then two things happened: my husband returned to the city and it began to rain.

It was clearly time to turn my attention to what I had thus far managed to avoid: the state of a house that had been empty for four months, a house with pine needles still on the floor and red candle wax on the upright piano and Christmas stock-ings on the doors and tissue paper strewn across the guest beds. It wasn't just the Christmas debris; that was insignifi-cant. It was the house itself.

The way we usually describe it to friends—"an old farmhouse" —implies a grace and coherence that we have never achieved and that was probably never there in the first place. My friend Brooke possesses what people think of when they think of an old farmhouse: a gracious two-story Victorian with a hand pump by the front door, wood neatly stacked on the porch, tall windows with the original wavy glass panes framed by tie-back curtains, and a screened-in porch where she and I drink iced tea and watch the kittens tumble at our feet.

This house of ours is something else—a house that we intended to become another but that became ours in a kind of inverse of squatters' rights. In our urgency to acquire certain necessities for the duration—water, for example—the house began to evolve in curious ways. The carpenter who worked with us would ask one morning, "Where do you want the door to the bathroom?" and then and there we would make a decision. Not having planned to renovate it in the first place, neither had we planned for the time and money it would take, so that when we got tired and ran out of money (which occurred at more or less the same time), we simply stopped and lived in it the way it was until we moved back to the city. We continue to do so today, although lately we sense that the house is slipping back slowly to its original state, evidence of entropy in the nature of things.

What this means in practical terms is that since we ripped out the living room ceiling but didn't replace it, the floor of my daughter's bedroom serves as the ceiling of the living room, and every time she jumps (and she and her friends are given to jumping) a century and a half of dirt falls between the boards and down upon the living room. It means that a film of ash from the wood stove (our only source of heat) covers every horizontal surface from November to April. It means having only hot water in the kitchen ever since the pipes burst one winter and a permanently locked front door ever since a high summer wind slammed it shut, tripping the antique lock. In short, what it means is that we live in a nineteenth-century farmhouse with twentieth-century standards of functionality and tidiness. It is a no-win situation.

I had announced to everyone that we'd wait until a rainy day came to tackle the house, and my rainy day had come. Under ordinary circumstances I would have been true to my word; in fact, I would have jumped the gun, for I feel happier in a tidy house than in a messy one. Perhaps the reason I didn't jump on this occasion had something to do with being alone in the house with two little girls whose concentration on their play (dress up, dolls, Clue) and indifference to their surroundings was contagious. Or perhaps it was because this was supposed to be my vacation, too. Or perhaps it was because of that momentary glimpse of the house as it really is that I had had upon entering. Whatever the reason, instead of marching forth with vacuum and dust mop, I sat down in the living room in front of the fire and made rag dolls with the girls.

Our conversation mostly took the form of progress reports ("I'm sewing his leg on now") and questions ("Do you like the name Kevin Malcolm?"), but when I look back on it I think the inconsequentiality of the conversation contributed to the feeling of intimacy. When lunchtime came, my daughter wandered into the kitchen and brought back a package of hot dogs, a package of buns, a bottle of ketchup, and a jar of mustard. We cooked the hot dogs in the wood-stove fire and followed them up with marshmallows toasted on forks. Then, leaving the lunch debris on the floor, where it joined the dollmaking debris, we returned to our project. We sang a little—"Bill Grogan's Goat" and "On Top of Spaghetti" and "Amazing Grace"—but mostly we just sewed and listened to the rain. It was then I had my epiphany: this is what it's like to feel at home, at home. This is the way children feel all the time. And very possibly men as well. And this is why the failure of others to share the responsibility for a house is so terrible: because it robs women of this experience.

I can count on one hand the occasions when I've experienced the house that way. There are the occasional evenings when I've had too much to drink and nothing—not heaps of laundry or stacks of dirty dishes or dust balls under the cabinet—will penetrate my euphoria. There are the times when our best friends come to visit and in the happiness of having them with us and the utter trust in their love and approval I don't give a damn about the house. And there are the times when I have just finished cleaning and everything looks terrific. But it isn't the same.

When you really feel at home, at home, the things are no longer your things but the house's things. The atmosphere is not something you've created but the house's very own atmosphere, into which you enter and from which you depart. A great weight is lifted. The house has a life of its own. And so do you.

Maybe it's asking too much to be able to feel this way once you're grown up. Maybe once you have adult responsibilities, the experience of feeling at home, at home, is a kind of grace, and you should just be happy when it happens and not go around trying to figure out how to get more. I don't think so, though. I think once we recognize what it is—relief from a sense of exclusive responsibility—we can claim it for ourselves, and give it to each other. And I think we should.

The Popcorn Bowl

CARROLL STONER

Of all the possessions I have hauled home from foreign ports, including the black Oaxaca pots that I packed in baskets in the outdoor market in southern Mexico, the thing I love the most is my popcorn bowl. It is an oversized wooden one that I lugged back from the jungles of Bolivia after I'd finally faced the fact that the first man I ever loved did not love me.

That bowl means a lot to me. My husband and children and I have popcorn two or three times a week, and every time I make a two-pan batch it exactly fills my bowl to the brim. I make popcorn in the same Revereware pan my mother used, and it turns out perfect every time. Over the years, this has amazed some of my friends, who either use a machine (we've tried them all and don't think one of them is as good as my pan) or they haven't perfected their own system for making popcorn, which in turn amazes me.

We use the oil-popping method, although for calories' sake we should be using a hot-air popper. But my attitude (though not my husband's) toward popcorn is that it is one of the luxuries in life, and like champagne, it must be consumed under nearly perfect conditions.

For popcorn, that means drizzled (but not drenched) with butter mixed with a little oil to prevent burning and sprinkled (lightly, but not too lightly) with salt.

The requisites for popcorn eating are looser than those for champagne drinking. Popcorn can be eaten while watching television, of course, but that demeans it as a pastime. It's better while watching a good rented movie from the comfort of your own sofa. It's okay in a movie theater, especially in one of the chains that proudly proclaim their use of real butter, as if that should get it a third star in the Michelin guide. It's excellent eaten warm while reading a good book, though you must take care not to get butter stains on the pages. Popcorn is a simple pleasure best suited to informal family gatherings, and I've noticed that my oversized bowl encourages even recalcitrant teenagers to talk while hanging around it.

Popcorn is my comfort food, and I have eaten it while grieving over situations far more serious than unrequited passion. But popcorn is versatile and wonderful for celebrations such as Christmas Eve, after the gifts have been opened. It is also excellent and unexpected at cocktail parties. It warms my heart to watch guests park themselves close to my popcorn-filled fishbowls, while, drink in hand, they eat their fill and scatter crumbs hither and yon. Popcorn is a great equalizer, and I don't mind. A carpet not up to popcorn is not worth its salt.

I learned the fishbowl-for-popcorn trick from Gloria Steinem when she wrote a magazine story about entertaining on a budget before she (and the rest of us) got liberated from such mundane thoughts. Those big, clear-glass bowls are fine for eating popcorn in company. But my wooden bowl is as nearly perfect as a popcorn bowl can be for all other times.

It is made of dense, heavy wood, unfinished but with a rich, low gloss that has come from years of having its interior coated with butter and oil. I once knew what kind of wood it was, but have forgotten the Spanish word and know only that it is related to mahogany. So rich is its finish now that the bowl leaves an oily ring when set on a table, I recently noticed. I'm relieved because maybe that means I can finally relax about the crack it developed many years ago.

Even as a young woman I knew enough not to wash wooden ware in soap and water. I followed directions that explained how to wipe them with paper towels after each use. But as the bowl began to acquire a slight oil buildup, I couldn't resist cleaning it once in a while with a sponge and a squeeze of dishwashing soap. And, I admit it, once or twice I immersed it in a sink full of sudsy water.

It was about this time that the bowl cracked. The crack was only a surface fissure, but it worried me deeply. Several times I propped the bowl on its side and let oil sit on the entire area surrounding the crack, hoping it would soak into the wood and prevent the crack from growing. Either that worked, or the flaw in the wood was not very deep, because it never got any worse.

The jungly fragrance I remember so clearly from the day I chose it becomes more pronounced as the wood ages. My ex-boyfriend, then a Peace Corps worker and now a lawyer with high-priced rock singer clients, took me to a tiny house in a clearing of the Bolivian jungle close to the Brazilian border. It was a sight I will never forget and I'm glad I didn't have a camera, though I wished for one at the time. A photograph would demean the strength of my memory. I think the sun couldn't quite make it through the roof of dense leaves over the edges of the clearing, but perhaps that's not accurate. I think the house had a thatched roof and that the woodworker's youngest son was five or six, completely naked and not circumcised. A picture would be wrong, making this memory too literal, too specific for my taste.

Now, I can both remember those years and see how my bowl has aged. The wood has darkened over the years but is still richly grained, with a range in color from pine yellow to mahogany. It is so hard that even a long-tined silver fork can't leave an impression in it. This I know from the many times I have eaten the last few pieces of soggy salad from its bottom. It is nicked and chipped around the top edge, the way a sturdy family utensil should be after years of hard use.

But the bowl's best feature is its fragrance. After each use, I still hold that bowl in front of my face with both hands, which is the only way I can hold it because of its weight, and inhale deeply of the faintly peppery, spicy smell that seems to intensify over the years and that is redolent of exotic, jungle romance, sensuous pleasures, and loss.

When I was still brokenhearted, the smell could bring a lump to my throat. After a while, the longing faded, and it finally ended when I told my former lover that the bowl had become a fixture in my life, and that my children and husband and I ate popcorn from it several times each week. "Popcorn?" he said, with a derisive tone in his voice and a questioning look on his face. In that look I saw layers of differences between us that would never have made for a peaceful home and family life, In short, we could never have spent twenty years together, developing a common history, eating popcorn.

Many people think popcorn is, well, déclassé, or perhaps simply . . . corny. My own New Yorker husband, at first, ate a polite handful or two to placate me but continued to regard popcorn as a nonfood and often wondered out loud who could prefer popcorn to a corned-beef sandwich.

With a family history that reached back to the steppes of Russia and the ghetto of Warsaw, he never had popcorn at home. My home was neither more nor less happy because of popcorn, but we ate it regularly on cold Minnesota nights (and warm ones) and we each learned to make it at a young age. I thought he had been deprived of an essential American family experience and vowed to convert him.

Recently he entertained us by reading aloud a newspaper story that told how the per capita consumption of popcorn was highest in—guess which state? Minnesota, home of progressive politics, white pines, and tough little kids who wade in the lakes carrying saltshakers for the leeches that curl up and fall off your feet when sprinkled with salt.

Over the years he has developed an affection for popcorn. Now, when we cluster around my big, beautiful bowl, he complains loudly if it's not within arm's length. He has learned that popcorn is not something to eat a few kernels of, but a food worthy of reflection—an evening's pastime. This is the kind of compromise upon which lives are built.

Bed

LAURA GREEN

If I had to boil domestic life down to its essence, reduce it to the one object that stands for it all, that object would have to be my bed, maybe even my side of the bed. I have been sharing this bed and its predecessor with the same man for seventeen years. I can't sleep on the left; he can't sleep on the right. After all these years, we both find it hard to sleep alone. I have gotten used to his body next to mine. It is my security, just as the bed is my secure place.

If it is true that home is where you feel the most comfortable, the place where people not only have to take you in but accept you for who you are, then the bedroom is the heart of my home, the place where I can be myself. I don't let just anyone into my bedroom any more than I would let just anyone into my bed.

Some can argue that the kitchen is the core of any happy family because people gather there. They'd have a point, of course. Our kitchen is busy, noisy, and public. My daughter and her friends bake cookies after school and sit at the counter eating them. My husband, who once sat at that same counter reading the papers while I cooked around him, now stands and chops onions to order. Baseball cards are sorted on the counter, hair is set and crimped there, fights are fought, allowances are doled out. Much of our life is acted around that little stage. But that's my point: the whole kitchen is a stage, a place where we have to accommodate, be polite, chew with our mouths closed, observe the basic niceties. True home is backstage, a place where you can unravel if that's what you feel like doing.

When we were moving in, I thought that the heart of our house would be the room I called the library because we put books in it. But because that's also where we keep the stereo, television, and VCR, the room is never empty. It's a place for absorbing what other people are thinking, not for figuring out your own thoughts. A library where you can sit and think would have a door on it and a desk in the middle, unlike our doorless, couch-filled room.

No, the heart of my house has to be my bed. If relaxation and acceptance are the warp and woof of domestic life, and if home is the place where I am most free to be myself, then my bed is the place where it all comes together. Here is where I think naked thoughts, daydream, make love, worry, plot, argue, get my back scratched, speculate, talk about growing old, and, finally, cut the mooring ties and drift out with the dream tide.

The bed, the place where we are born and die, is our primeval place, the place our children claim instinctively. That is why they run to my bed when they are sick, when they need to study for a test, when they want to cry, when they can't sleep and need comfort.

Therein lies the problem of the family bed. It does not give much privacy. Our bed isn't all that big, and I had thought it would be too small for big kids to feel welcome in it. Nonsense. They march in like conquerors and flop down, assuming that we will roll over—and we do. Some mornings I lie there, as straight as a toothpick, because I have no room to curl up.

When my old bed, which I had dragged from apartment to apartment, up and down a dozen narrow staircases, wore out, my husband and I thought hard about its replacement—how big it should be, how firm the mattress, what sort of embellishments it should have. We overlooked the social aspects.

When I was between marriages, I wanted a double bed because I thought it was the perfect size for a single woman. It's big enough to roll around in without feeling straightjacketed, the way you do when you spend a night in a twin bed after years in something bigger. There's room for overnight guests, but not so much room that they feel comfortable enough to entertain thoughts of returning soon with their laundry. A double bed is snug enough that a small woman sleeping alone can warm it up in less than an hour, something to think about on a frigid February night in Chicago.

Unfortunately, a double bed is best for the single life. Over the long haul, it is too narrow to accommodate a husband. One of my old friends and her husband used to sleep in a double bed with a permanent trough in the middle. No matter how they tried, they always rolled into each other. She said that being nine months pregnant in a double bed was an experience she wouldn't wish on a dog. I'm not implying cause and effect, but they are no longer married.

A king-sized bed was out of the question for us. Back then we lived in little apartments in old brownstones. If we had put a king-sized bed in one of those tiny rooms, it would have taken up so much space that we wouldn't have been able to open the bottom dresser drawers all the way. I didn't want to think of what it would be like huffing and shoving one of those mattresses up two flights of angled, rickety brownstone back porch stairs, either. Dealing with babies and baskets of laundry was bad enough.

So we brought a queen, even though my husband is six-two and would have been happy to loll about on something grander. The difference between a queen and a king isn't much, but that hand span makes a big difference when you're angry and don't know how to make up. Call me a pessimist if you want for worrying about ending fights before we even married, but we are late-night squabblers. I thought that if we, who are sullen and touchy, had to sleep in a queen-sized bed, we wouldn't be able to help brushing up against each other after our fights. If we touched, it would be harder to stay sulky. And that's the way it has worked, except when I am so furious that sharing a bed seems like sleeping with the enemy. Then I stalk off to the spare room and brood in a narrow old twin.

Deciding on a bed was easier than picking sheets. For one thing, there were fewer choices. We got married about the time fancy sheets started coming on the market. Tightwad that I am, I had been sleeping on perfectly good, dowdy white sheets. Since he had agreed not to make the bed with his avocado green sheets, which were the exact color of a sixties refrigerator, and since he had reluctantly thrown out his ex-wife's fake leopard-skin throw, I allowed as how we could get some print sheets. In deference to my supposedly advanced design sense, he said he would do without pastel stripes. Respecting his masculine sensibilities, I took a pass on ruffles. We compromised on Finnish prints in defiant primary colors.

We built a boxy platform for the mattress. That way, I never had to sweep the floor. Above the bed, we hung a phallic Oldenburg print that all but snickered. I thought we were stylish and clever, but the illusion fled when I saw the same print in a suburban kitchen, next to some ceramic chickens and a beribboned basket filled with dried flowers.

We grew older and moved the bed to a house with a tiny back bedroom, which it nearly fills. We surrounded it with stacks of books and magazines. We put the Oldenburg down in the basement and bought lots of pillows so we could prop ourselves up and read before we went to sleep.

Ours was a good nest, but we have all but outgrown it. The children and the dog still crawl in, although the children are getting bigger and the dog is getting older. I worked hard for my secure, private corner, and I alternately love and hate sharing it with them. It's joyous to have them hug and kiss me. It's hell to be sucked into a discussion at six in the morning. It's a demonstration of their love. It's an invasion of my privacy. Sometimes I feel that mine is a domesticity run amok.

There is the domesticity of those who always live alone and can make a precise nest with only the objects they want in it. There is the domesticity of those who finally find a place of their own and gratefully settle into it. There is the domesticity of the family, a noisy, compromising state so ingrained that I barely can remember how much I enjoyed living by myself. At its core is my bed, my refuge. When I am drowsing in the dark, in the depths of my old bed in the back of my house, when I know the children are asleep in their beds and the dog is curled up on the floor next to me, I am entirely at home in a setting as familiar and disheveled as an old bathrobe.

Maybe that's why I am uncomfortable in almost every adult's bedroom but my own. I feel like a spy when I see his tie snaked across the dresser atop her watch, her earrings mixed up with his pocket change, lotion bottles and old belt buckles, a pen, paper clips and scraps of paper, all in conjugal disarray, entwined in offhand intimacy, like bodies under the covers. I want to leave quickly and I do. It's like wearing someone else's underwear.

There is a moment at the end of the day when it really is the end of the day. The children are asleep. Our reading time— ten minutes if it has been an exhausting day, a half hour if

not—is ending. The print is swimming before my eyes. My
husband's eyes are shutting, the lids as delicate as a baby's. I
reach behind me and turn out the light, and in that wonderful
dreamy state between sleep and awareness, we curl up around
each other, secure as puppies in a basket. It is the best part of
the day.

Oh, how we have struggled to achieve this. How many
fights! How many tears! How many reconciliations! We are
not ready to share it with just anybody.

Mornings

NANCY EBERLE

During our first year of living on a farm (a five-year adventure
from which we have long since returned), we had no plumbing
and no running water. We had an outhouse. It was a classic of
its kind. It had flaked and peeling red paint (what was left of
it) and overweathered wood, it was malodorous even after
years of disuse, and where there should have been a door, it
had an unimpeded view of Iowa perhaps some twenty miles
distant, across the Mississippi River Valley.

Since the first part of that first year was harsh winter—deep
snow covered by a surface crust of glare ice, 20-below temper-
atures, howling winds—I won't pretend the lack of plumbing
wasn't difficult. The middle-of-the night runs were the worse,
as we roused ourselves from the warmth around the wood
stove to make a mad dash out into the frigid and starlit night
and back again. Second-worst were the early-morning trips,

the normal urgency now a matter of desperation, due to the work of the night's cold on bladder and kidneys or whatever it is that responds to cold in that fashion.

But neither was life with an outhouse without its benefits. It got you *out*, and with a three-year-old to boot, which as everyone knows is no mean trick in the midst of winter. It got us out in brilliantly sunshiny, crackly cold days, and in blizzards so furious one of us went with the other for safety. It got us out on moonlit nights so beautiful that, once exposed, we donned our cross-country skis and went clattering across the icy crust, giggling like children. It got us out to enjoy the weather—no, to *experience* the weather, the elements, the very world to which we so easily forget we belong. It reminded us periodically, throughout the day, that we were part of that world. All of this by way of saying something about mornings, for which many people bear approximately the same affection that they bear for outhouses. To me, mornings are the best part of the day. I don't ordinarily go around trying to proselytize people to my point of view, and I don't intend to do so here. There are morning people and there are night people, and may they both prosper. My remarks are addressed to that broad band of uncommitted people, with the sole purpose of presenting for their consideration the concept that by reclaiming morning they may enlarge the dimensions of their day by a good fifth or so.

The morning I am talking about has no fixed dimensions—it is simply that which is currently being slept through. What is so wonderful about it? My mother had a phrase for it: "getting a jump on the day." What she meant, of course, was having time to establish your own priorities before facing the demands of others. In point of fact, she got her own jump on the day late the night before, sitting at her desk, a yellow legal pad before her. But nothing will ever convince me that half an hour at the end of one day is as good as half an hour at the beginning of the next.

What is so special about morning is peace—a deep sense of

being at home in one's self and one's house. There is no other time of day like it. It doesn't matter how the time is spent—it can be spent doing the dishes from the night before, as far as that goes. What makes it special is being alone in your own house. Some spend it making lists, some in making breakfast; some read the newspaper, others ride an exercise bike or meditate. What you do with the time doesn't matter; what's important is having it to yourself. (That's not entirely true. There is a large difference between time spent reading the newspaper, which is also time spent in oblivion of one's self and might just as well be spent in sleep, and time spent in a more contemplative manner.) The key to morning time well spent is any activity that allows you to—in the words of the gurus—"be here now." Or more simply put, to pay attention. The wonderful thing about such time is that you get double your money. The peacefulness you experience during morning hours is there to come back to again at any time throughout the day, whereas it is nearly impossible to find once you have hurtled from bed to full involvement. So what we are talking about is consciousness, being conscious of who you are and where you are before (I am tempted to say before all hell breaks loose)—before the day with all its demands gets the jump on you. And that's what makes it worth getting up for.

Dollhouses

CARROLL STONER

Dolls yes, dollhouses no. I had decided that early on. We were the generation who could raise our daughters without the influences that shape women into second-class citizens. I would buy dolls for Eve; after all, I wanted her to get practice in playing with a baby. But she would also have trucks and big building blocks and the kind of toys that encourage adventurous thinking and hand-eye coordination. Instead of a miniature iron and ironing board, she'd have an Erector set.

And after reading a study about how boy toddlers build towers while girls build enclosures, how boys build extravagant edifices while girls hurriedly build minimally constructed rings of blocks so they can have tea parties inside, I decided she would never, under any circumstances, have a dollhouse.

Why present her with such an obvious symbol of staying home when the world was out there waiting for her? If the phallic symbol of tall, aggressive towers meant adventure, I reasoned, then the enclosure or dollhouse was tied to feminine pursuits like decorating and cleaning and cooking, which all take place while containing oneself, literally and figuratively, inside the home. Then, too, the dollhouse seemed like a training ground for acquisitiveness. Did I want to raise a girl who obsessed about getting the right lamp for the right table in the right corner of the perfect room?

The first challenge to my decision came when we bought a

country house. It was more a cottage than a real home, tiny and cozy, and we knew instinctively it would provide genuine pleasure for our family. Surrounded by woods and meadows, it spoke to something deep inside our family that craved peace and quiet and small-scale projects we could do with our hands and finish in an afternoon.

Our plans were to improve the place little by little. This house was no major architectural project with walls to be moved or skylights to be installed. And so it evolved, until soon it began to feel like home. We slept soundly after seeing more stars in the country sky than we knew existed. We awoke to birdcalls. Inside, two sofas were built and covered in blue-and-white pillow ticking, and miscellaneous rockers in various stages of disrepair were fixed and cushioned in chintz.

The house began to take on character. Pitchers covered a tabletop. Tatted and crocheted lace filled baskets. Butter churns were clustered in a corner. Bathroom window curtains matched a rose wallpaper border that I applied with Elmer's glue in a spare half hour. Old, handmade baby dresses hung from miniature wooden hangers on a wall. Some of these were fancy enough for a christening. Others were made of durable cotton, from a time when baby girls wore dresses every day.

No matter where I was in the cottage, my surroundings gave me pleasure. Nothing was expensive. The house was a hodgepodge of furniture and accessories—nothing matched anything else. And yet there was something indefinably cohesive about it. There were the beginnings of a family history within the walls, but that wasn't it. The summer-pastel colors were cheery even on a gloomy winter day, but that wasn't what gave me such feelings of pride.

Then one day I saw that the furnishings had one thing in common: they were unmistakably feminine, in the traditional sense of pink and blue and patterned prints. And the collections, to a last one, symbolized "women's work." We'd done most of it ourselves, from idea through execution. We'd loved almost every minute of it. This was our dollhouse.

Early on the bright winter morning of my discovery, before my daughter awoke, I planned our day. I would staple-gun new fabric to some chair seats. I would make a pot of chicken soup for Sunday lunch and to freeze. Together, we would count the minutes while she baked her first cornmeal muffins. Then we would eat them the way my mother taught us to, warm from the oven with butter and maple syrup.

What we would do, in short, was play house.

I thought of my late mother with a mixture of affection and regret, recognizing how little I knew her when she was alive. My mother loved to bake, though preparing daily meals bored her silly. I've reversed the preference, loving to make anything I can prepare without a recipe and hating to follow the precise directions required by baking. She sewed beautifully—a prom gown of dark iridescent taffeta with an overskirt of black tulle, curtains made of sheets back when that was new, the height of cleverness. She arranged and rearranged our living room furniture. She recovered chairs, painted bookcases, and then started all over again. She loved her house. She drove me wild.

One day, after deciding it was her duty to teach her daughters how to keep house, she made a series of lists that explained how to clean each room. There was one list for the kitchen, one for bathrooms, and one for bedrooms ("First, remove everything from the closet floor"). I saw those lists as a classic example of her elevation from house proud to house crazy.

I attributed her devotion to our home to the fact that she had nothing better with which to occupy her mind. I feared that if I found pleasure in the same things she did, I might also become "just a housewife." And so the pleasure I found in sewing and cooking stayed secret for decades, while I found comfort in climbing the corporate ladder. That was real work. Those other homely skills seemed connected to things in women's pasts, like baton-twirling and using three shades of blue eyeshadow—things women like us just don't do any more.

Times have changed. There are worlds out there to con-

quer. Who wants to keep baby girls in dresses, so that when
they crawl, they move up the insides of the dresses until the
collars choke them and they fall, face forward, onto the floor?
Who wants home-sewn prom gowns?

I have come full circle in my attitudes toward women's
work. First I loved it and did it myself. Then I left it to
someone else, often someone who had no real interest in my
home or life. I was aware of every undone task and hated the
very thought of having to monitor someone else's work, or of
doing it myself, or of having to nag everyone in my family to
share, please, just a little of it. I ignored it. I hated it. I loved
it.

So what has all of this to do with building phallic towers
and womblike enclosures? I like my womb, what little I know
of it. I love my home, though it does not define me. There
may have been a time when I confused the ability to create a
comfortable and beautiful and orderly home with the silliest
kind of decorating—like those three shades of eyeshadow.
And yes, if boys are allowed to wander far from home on their
bicycles while girls are warned to keep their dresses clean,
then our horizons will be closer to home and our dreams more
modest.

But I have learned that the work that goes into homemaking
is as important to my satisfaction as any work I've ever done.
Is the home an outlet for creativity? Of course it is. Are the
home and family sources of challenge? Do they provide the
pleasure of achievement? Absolutely. Is the home the site of
simple pleasures that are as enjoyable as more complex, intellectual activities? Of course.

But is there scut work in homemaking? Sure, and to the
extent that I can pay to have it done, I will. But there's junk
attached to every job—even corporate presidents have to work
at the details of keeping it all afloat. Homemaking itself,
and this I know, is as satisfying as a carefully chosen career.
Do I want, then, to be a full-time housewife? No more than
I want to give up the stimulation of city life for the peace

of my country cottage. I want them both. They balance each other.

How can we imbue women's work with a sense of dignity? By taking it seriously and by doing it with pleasure. And if there's no appreciation for women's work? Who cares? Some things we do for ourselves.

As for that dollhouse for my daughter, I'll reconsider.

Produce

NANCY EBERLE

I'm a pushover for produce. Not the kind I find in my neighborhood supermarket, where pretension (morels from Moravia, beets from Belgravia, carrots the size of radishes, green beans the size of garter snakes) has long ago outstripped common sense. No, the produce that calls to me calls from foreign neighborhoods instead of foreign climes. It calls from corner stores where banners proclaim in ecstatic, foot-high red letters, "Lettuce! Three for $1!" and "Cantaloops Just Arrived!" In those stores, rows of leeks demand their own Cézanne and bing cherries gleam with windows of light; blushing turnips, sensuous eggplants, creamy cauliflowers, fingers of parsnip, and fragrant cantaloupes are all, all in a state of such perfection that you feel you are among the ur-fruits of the earth.

If the chic supermarket is distinguished by its foreign produce, then the serious produce market is distinguished by its foreign customers. Women in babushkas sort through the zucchini with the grim concentration of quality-control workers.

Bleached blonds of a certain age discuss in rich accents the price of the perfect spans of bananas clutched in their heavily ringed fingers. Sallow old women with coarse dark hair and shapeless black dresses add still more tomatoes to those already in their plastic bags, all the while carrying on a conversation. The work is done by the hands, as when a kennel club judge runs his hands down a Pomeranian's back even while he's talking to the owner.

As soon as I enter such a store, the serpent strikes—the serpent in this case being gluttony. I, who buy perhaps half a dozen peaches and one sack of cherries per season, begin to fill my cart with peaches and cherries, grapes and pears, as if there were no tomorrow. I, who eat vegetables with neither prejudice nor pleasure (except for sweet corn, of course), amass broccoli upon cauliflower upon kale upon spinach.

The spirit of largesse abroad in this store is infectious. I dispense plastic bags to little old ladies who can't reach them, retrieve a rolled-away orange, tell a handsome, dark-haired stock boy how beautiful everything is, and venture my opinion on the best kind of potato salad (sliced new potatoes, layered with sour cream, bacon, and onions).

When I leave this Eden to enter the River Styx of the check-out counter, I feel myself and my purchases undergo a kind of shrinking. I have a lot of food—five times the amount of produce I usually buy—but it suddenly looks puny when detached from the displays all around me. I eye my neighbors' baskets, watching as they unload their choices. As the woman with the coarse black hair and tomato-wise hands hoists her sack, I picture her standing before her stove, stirring a vat of tomato sauce with a wooden spoon. I see her voluble extended family around the table, lots of adults, lots of children, reaching, laughing, arguing, helping themselves to more. It seems to me that such a woman knows these fruits of the earth in an intimate way I can never aspire to. I am the foreigner here, and although our baskets are filled with the same fruits, hers will be the sweeter.

When I get home I set the bags on the kitchen counter and clean out the crisper before unloading them. The first night I make an enormous green and white salad for dinner using the snow-white mushrooms, the crisp zucchini, the broccoli that I made bright by blanching, the cool cucumbers and the crunchy cauliflower. I dress it with a lime-curry dressing—the rich gold is almost shocking against all those cool tones. The next night I make a vegetable soup with the tomatoes, potatoes, carrots, turnips, parsley, and basil and throw in some pinto beans, pasta, and Parmesan for good measure. The next night we go out. The night after that we get home late so we order in: pizza.

As the week goes on, the parsnips shrivel, the spinach grows slimy, and the last six cherries shrink in shame. Perhaps what I love is not produce at all, but a particular kind of beauty— the beauty of bounty, of plenty. The beauty of sixty eggplants hip to hip in gravid purple, the pointy green stars around their necks like the fastenings of cloaks. Or perhaps it's not bounty, but simply what the lavish hand, like the ecstatic red signs, enables the eye to see: the loveliness that lies in everyday things.

Full-Time Mother

MARY BETH DANIELSON

From the day we start kindergarten, life draws us out of our houses. School, college, jobs—to learn you go out. To grow up you go out. To live you go out.

Now that I'm thirty-six and a mother to two small children.

I stay home. When I can find or arrange some hours to write,
I do. But most of the hours of most of my days I mother my
kids. The brilliance of the morning sun pours into my living
room, and I'm the adult here to see it. The house is filled with
sounds, but they are all kid sounds: tinny children's TV, chattering and squabbling, the clatter of toys falling against each
other. I stand at the door of the kitchen and look to see if they
are okay. What I see is the kids, sunlight spilling over their
heads. They are beautiful. I adore them. But because of them
my daytime world is the limbo of full-time parenting.

Should a woman work outside her home or stay home to be
with her kids? The question, so important, also seems so
petty. The world is filled with a million starving children. It
seems cranky and Alice-in-Wonderlandish to rage at middle-
class American women about the child-care arrangements they
make. If those child-care prophets are so worried, shouldn't
they harangue someone about skeletal children lying on rags at
the corners of the earth?

Some people are good parents, some dreadful whether they
work at home or outside it. Some children will thrive with
parents who work outside the home, some will accommodate,
some will fail. There simply isn't an equation that proves one
environment is sterile, the other rich.

So, you ask, why am I here?

I once read Jung's answer when asked why he went to
Africa: "I wanted to see how it would affect me." In many
ways, my reason for staying home with my kids is the same. If
we are human animals, looking for wisdom, then parenting is
one of the most spiritual tasks we attempt in our lives. It is
primal, ancient, unnerving, requiring, and therefore it builds
patience, imagination, and grace. It is part of that inward
journey mystics and hippies talk about. At times it requires
more devotion than even saints have. It is wearing a hair shirt.

Parenting forces us to deal with our own childhoods. I was a
kid well raised—but not cherished. My parents loved and
provided the best they could for their three children. They

took us to church five times a week and read the Bible to us after supper. I was clean, fed, and provided with toys, music, a dog, my own bedroom, and thirty acres of field and woods in which to spin myself out. But they were never generous with praise. My parents seemed to believe special attention or encouragement would make for uppity children.

In the pilgrimage of raising my own kids, much of my anger has dissolved; I am being healed. When I hug my kids and tell them I love them, the little girl in me gets hugged, too. My anger turns to grief for that long-gone little girl bursting her heart to please Mommy and Daddy. And grief for my kind and hard-working parents, who never understood that they were adored. I could not bear to not be here for my little kids now. The little girl in me who felt abandoned could not stand it.

My husband's family also looked picture-perfect but the truth was that his parents were alcoholics and his upbringing was painful. Our memories are the foundation of this decision we made about the direction our lives would take. All adults have private griefs and strengths from childhood that affect everyday life. We have to remember what it felt like to be a kid, to remember what both love and alienation felt like. Then we do our intelligent best to shape our children's world accordingly.

I am also here because my husband and I are card-carrying feminists.

I want my children to grow up to be tolerant, radical, and feminist. Maybe it won't work; I'm well aware I didn't grow up to be the person my parents wanted me to be. But I do have an insider's understanding of my parents' life and a respect for their commitment. It's more difficult in a pluralistic society to hand strong values and beliefs on to our kids. My husband and I can't and don't expect others besides ourselves to take this work seriously.

I love the person Lilly is and who she is becoming. My husband and I joke, with amazement and respect, that she is our "Innate Princess." For the first two years of her life we dressed her in brightly colored overalls. When she learned how to talk she asked for a pink dress. She is many things, but what most people notice first is her careful, docile, "feminine" ways. It has been a challenge for both my husband and me to let her be who she is while at the same time encouraging and enticing her into activities she might not begin on her own. She learns to use blocks and balls and to splash through puddles when it rains, and we assure her over and over again that it's okay to get dirty, that clothes wash. Nothing about this is dramatic. Yet now, at four years old, when she climbs eight feet high on the monkey bars, hangs on to an overhead bar, and kicks out with her feet, I am satisfied. When she comes in from "building houses" with mud and scrap lumber, dirt streaked across her face and clothes, I'm pleased. For three years I kept hearing people say what a good girl she was. The other day, for the first time, someone called her a tomboy. I don't like labels, but I do understand the realities that underlie them and am convinced that being here with my kids, in the long run, means some of my values will get through to them and into their lives.

I don't do this alone. My husband and I are a team. I do the lioness's share of daytime parenting around here, but the reality that keeps us going is that we have both made sacrifices to rear our children in this way. This means that when Max cries in the middle of the night, as he usually does, my husband is the one who gets up to tend to him. Either of us is likely to toss the laundry in the washer; either of us is likely to forget to take it out of the dryer; either of us is accountable for the wrinkled clothes we often wear. Both of us volunteer at our daughter's preschool, both of us make medical appointments for the kids and take them there. Our "time together" is when we finish supper dishes, after we've put the kids to bed.

Our decision to make sacrifices for our children means that when the opportunity arose, my husband chose to continue his career on a free-lance basis. Now he leaves our house late in the morning to go to work and comes home at dinner. Then, after the children are in bed, if he has more work to do, he does it. It's not uncommon for him to work until two or three o'clock in the morning.

I'm not an angry person and it's a good thing, because an angry person probably couldn't do this with grace. It *is* self-sacrificing to stay home, mind kids, and lead them gently through their small ways. If I were doing this alone, if my husband expected to come home, be served dinner, and then sit down to watch TV or read, I would explode. Our life would no longer be something we are giving our children; it would be a life I was giving my husband.

Still, I clutch. Every day there are moments that throw me, when who I try to be stumbles over what I am doing. Those moments are unsettling, sometimes frightening.

For instance, my husband is ready to leave for work. He gives me a fifteen-minute warning that he's leaving. I get up from the chair in the office where I've been writing for several hours. I walk out, close the door. My children run to cling to me and my brain reels. The phrases that were dancing in my mind scatter and fall away. I remember that what I do now is wash and dress the kids, think about groceries and errands and play dates. I will be with these kids for the next eight or nine hours and my own longings must spin back to beginner speed.

I often pull both children in a heavy wagon for a mile to a McDonald's for lunch then pull them back home. I take them on the bus and the el to the zoo, to visit friends at their houses, to meet "downtown" friends for luncheon dates at business-district restaurants. We go to museums, to a favorite fancy playground in a distant neighborhood, to a crowded city beach on hot summer mornings. I've taken them with me to political demonstrations and to volunteer stints at a shelter for homeless women. I'm proud of these adventures, but I also realize they often arise out of an ambiguity and panic. The sun is shining out there, I want to get out, go someplace, exhaust myself at something beyond laundry and Candyland.

Every day, when I take my children outside, I unlatch the gate and they tumble out like puppies. We amble to the right or we amble to the left, looking for neighborhood friends. Lilly stops under trees to see if she can touch the bottom branches yet. She picks dandelions. Max picks up stones and throws them in the street, squealing past the pacifier in his mouth. I am a simple parent, delighted by my children's delight. Their unconscious cuteness tickles my solar plexus.

Their joy at discovering the world is a bell, ringing and reverberating inside me. It jars memories from my girlhood. I remember, so intensely that I almost reexperience it, the possibilities in a tree. I might try to climb it, or play house under it, or collect the free, abundant leaves. I could make a spyglass out of my cupped hands, stare up into the branches and let the world spin into a brilliant, light-suffused green.

But some days the snail's pace, the smallness of my children's world rankles. I see over their heads to the end of the block. I know what lies beyond. I want to go fast, to see something curious and new. Instead I am rooted to this small street. I feel like someone has crammed a bowl over my head and now insists it must be my horizon.

Like I said, I'm thirty-six. Old enough to know what I'm missing. Old enough to know what I have.

Unholy Angels

LAURA GREEN

The angel was barely noticeable, obscured by a crowd of black clay donkeys, owl whistles, jaguars, and other creatures making up the peasant menagerie in the market stall on the outskirts of Oaxaca. Her face was pressed from a Victorian mold; it was a sentimental, realistic European face with a pug nose and a prissy circle of a mouth. Her body was more an exercise in Indian geometry than an evocation of anything fleshy. She had two U-shaped clay coils for arms. Her wings were oval slabs, as alert as rabbit ears. Her dress and body were shaped into a simple hollow cone. As I lifted her, the clapper rang with a dull, metallic treble, and I realized the angel was also a bell. Function, form, and ideal rolled into one. I bought her.

The marriage between human and abstract is what an angel is about. Angels aren't all of a piece. They're mediators between worlds, neither here nor there. They are not crude enough for earth but too much like it to belong anywhere else. They are Blake's creatures, intense and feeling beings. Fiery shapes, flickering, as orgasmic as Bellini's St. Teresa in ecstasy. So I own a few angels.

I'm not an organized collector, although I am a peerless accumulator. Most collecting seems prissy and entirely beside the point, as if it were important to have objects in quantity when what you really want is one or two things that mean a lot. I am all for souvenirs, stuff that brings back moments. But collecting is all too often just gathering up stuff.

Angels may be an exception to the rule that too many collections are studies in cuteness by people who would bristle at being called cute. I know an accomplished scientist who collects little doggies. My cousin collects apples, right down to the apple magnets on her refrigerator. I have an old friend who collected frogs, not real frogs but photos, paintings, and needlepoints of green, spotted bullfrogs. She once hung a needlepoint of bug-eyed humping frogs over her downstairs toilet, a confounding statement. I even know someone with several collections, hardly any of them cute, an accomplishment that took some doing and a lot of weekends at flea markets. She began by collecting kitchen equipment with asparagus on it, particularly Italian faience asparagus plates, a collection that was handsome enough to be photographed for a home furnishings magazine. After her divorce, she said she had always hated asparagus and had started collecting for her husband. So she switched to hand-crafted furniture, and folk paintings and carvings for reasons of her own. I have met women who collect onyx mushrooms and women who save up for Quimper platters and women who buy little wooden owls with big yellow eyes. In yet another fit of domestic conformity, when I felt I was being too work-oriented, I started buying pitchers. I hate to use the word *collect*, since I was so sheepish about it. Collectors are proud. I have an abortive collection by now, mostly the wrong size and too many brown ones. I have an offhand assembly of cloth art, Hmong textiles, a Cree felt collage, and a Panamanian trapunto panorama of women planting cotton. It's not a thought-out collection but rather the result of a desire to own something made by other women.

With a few exceptions, men don't collect, at least not the way women do. My neighbor across the alley, a lawyer who likes to tell people he just met that he went to Harvard Law School, is a stamp collector. But his is a deliberate, expensive, aggressive kind of collecting. He has made an investment.

Like a rare-book collection, also kept under glass and under wraps, his collection has a dollar value.

For women, collecting is a nonprofit affair. Women buy pussycats or cookie jars or tureens the way little boys buy baseball cards. We go for quantity, casting the net wide and often. Like my son, who paws through the baseball-card value books, we think it would be nice if we struck gold. Profit would be a bonus; resale value is beside the point. Women fill the cupboards and the countertops with trinkets the way nature fills a field with plants and for the same reason. We hate a vacuum.

The idea of filling a vacuum with angels, though, is nice, a bit like putting fireflies in a bottle. I now own two angels in addition to the Oaxacan black angel. I have a putto that looks a lot like a five-year-old who lives on my block, although an angel as tough and independent as she is would have been tumbled down to hell ages ago. And there's my wooden Balinese angel, half human and half Indonesian bird god, my protector. Her wings are carved with stylized feathers painted gold and gaudy pink. Her left leg dangles lazily down through the gap in her sarong. A slip of the woodcarver's knife has left her cockeyed and slightly pug-nosed. My husband bought her for me at the end of a week-long trip after he awoke one morning surprised and a bit relieved to realize that, after all these years, he still missed me.

Angels are worth collecting because they are worth thinking about. For those of us who are skeptics, angels are more palatable than God. God is forbidding, judgmental, fair, inflexible, untemptable, and impersonal. Angels are sensuous, sympathetic creatures, fallible and subject to temptation.

We are drawn to angels, and I would like to think they are drawn to us. What could be more erotic than making love to a fiery, ephemeral angel? Perhaps making love to a fallen angel who could be distracted from his anguish only by getting lost in sex. Think of their beautiful Biblical names—Raphael, Gabriel, Uriel, Michael—and of their ability to see through us and know us. Think of falling asleep with an angel, wrapped up in his arms and legs, in a cocoon of soft wings.

Obviously I do not appreciate angels for their religious value. I'd just as soon think about them as wonderful figments of the imagination. They are a heroic attempt to put a face on a somewhat terrifying Biblical God, a compromise between our insubstantial selves and an inconceivably eternal presence. I like to see them as grand flourishes of the mind, not as the guardians of little children. My angels aren't cute felt creatures with pink circle cheeks and yellow yarn braids; they're Renaissance creatures with rainbow-colored feathers. I keep them around because they testify to our glorious human penchant for making something of nothing, for shrinking the terrible void of doubt, as proof of our delightful need to embellish life with glorious symbols.

When I am sitting on the floor, feet to the fire, and I look up and see an angel hanging from the ceiling, I think about human spirit and imagination. How could such a world be found in a little glass apple?

Mom

LAURIE ABRAHAM

I wrote my name across my mother's dresser this Christmas, LAURIE, in a thick layer of dust she never would have countenanced when I was a child. The dresser sits in her fourth home in twenty-five years of adulthood. She and my stepfather could afford the old two-story only because it's a mess:

the interior has been ravaged by hackneyed repair jobs and countless coats of bland green paint, the exterior ignored. Restoring the home's lost charm will take five years of weekends spent sanding, staining, painting, and then sanding some more.

For now, only three rooms are habitable, and no matter how often they are swept and dusted, the grime of rehabbing makes them filthy by the standards of the mother I grew up with. This woman taught me in the first grade the "right" way to clean the bathroom, a meticulous process that must be a family secret; I've yet to see it duplicated. A few key rules: Spray Vanish in the toilet bowl right off so it has time to soak before you attack with the brush; use Comet for the porcelain sink but not the countertop because it scratches; scrub the sink last because you need it to rinse the sponge while you're working on the toilet and tub (the dirty sponge, of course, would mess up the sink you've already cleaned). And so on. I often wonder how my mother survives the disarray of her new old home. Sometimes, she tells me, she doesn't think she will.

"Over the years I've given up so many of the things I used to do." She sounds plaintive but slightly proud.

Homes No. 1 and No. 2, one in Columbus, Indiana, the other in Columbus, Ohio: Although hundreds of miles apart, the first two homes belonged in spirit to the same neighborhood. One-story ranches with brick fronts and aluminum sides, they each claimed a patch of grass in a row of similar colonials, split-levels, and ranches. Their yards were cropped and green, with trim bushes and trees that knew their places. Crowded and uniform perhaps, but these "starter" neighborhoods had enough space, enough variety to suggest that this suburb's inhabitants could soon afford to build an addition, sink a swimming pool, or better yet, move. In my nine years in suburban Indiana and Ohio, I learned that mothers cook delicious dinners, sew Halloween costumes and matching dresses for their daughters and their daughters' dolls, wax floors four times a year, and play bridge. My mother was affectionate and supportive, strong almost to the point of stoicism. As a child, I saw her cry only once, sitting at the sewing machine, working the pedal, coaxing the fabric under the needle with both hands. She told me not to worry. I was scared.

"Monday, that was wash day," she remembers. "Tuesday was ironing; if I was really lucky I finished part of it the night before. Wednesday, I was sort of off; I did big cleaning jobs or a special craft project." Like the wicked witch with the stiff burlap dress and gray, glued-yarn hair. "Thursday was groceries, and Friday, I would clean the whole house, work until it was time to cook dinner for your father. Now I hardly ever wax furniture, even though I know how good furniture dries out in winters like these." She looks toward the heavy wood bookshelves that haven't been waxed since they arrived five years ago with my stepfather.

Then she stands and removes a smudge from the coffee table with the edge of her blue terry robe and smooths a bulge in the throw rug at the back door. "My ideal, I wanted everything to be just so. . . . Just so. That phrase keeps coming to my head. I wanted things to be new and shiny. We wanted to have a place we were proud of, like in the magazines and all that—people with college degrees, your father in business, blah, blah, blah."

She moves to the bookshelves, which hold a Mexican mask I gave her for Christmas and a diary she has never written in, to adjust a fan of books into a more perfect fan. "My only place to accomplish anything was with you guys and the house. I was somebody because everybody said I kept such a beautiful home and because you wore such beautiful clothes. In those days I thought, Oh, my God, I'll never work again. I'll never be anyone who has any responsibility. I always feared the future, what would happen when you guys were gone."

Home No. 3, Mentor, Ohio: Hanging from my father's pin-striped coattails as he jumped the corporate ladder, my mother, sister, and I next landed on Hidden Hollow Drive, a looping path festooned with the cul-de-sacs that mark a true

suburb and removed from the grid of streets. Our home was
the two-story my sister and I had long coveted; it would have
been perfect with the station wagon or Winnebago we were
never able to persuade our parents to buy. Our yard was
larger than before—almost an acre, I told my friends—and it
backed into woods thick enough to obscure the street on the
other side.

My mother started her first full-time work since I was born
in this place, using the master's degree in guidance and counseling she had quietly earned while her bachelor's degree in
home economics kept our home humming. We got our first
cleaning lady during these years—our first *three* cleaning ladies, to be precise, because no one did the job right until Myrt
Pickett came along. Meanwhile, my mother proved to herself
that she could succeed in the working world but that she could
not love my father any more.

Today, she doesn't have much to say about that two-story
house she so carefully designed with the builder, picking out
wallpaper, flooring, and fixtures for every room: "Mentor—
the house was a place to leave."

Home No. 4, Cleveland Heights, Ohio: Three and a half
rooms renovated, nine to go. Despite the work ahead, my
mother calls her current home her favorite. "Now I know I
can make it on the job. The house is my haven, somewhere to
come to, to recuperate, get some warmth and be taken care
of."

She picks bits of lint from her chair with one hand and
collects them in the other. "My friend Dan says this place has
warmth. I feel good about that. I feel like I'm preserving
something by renovating this old place. And I wanted enough
space, a full extra bath, so I could entertain you with some
amount of ease. That's important to me," she says.

My mother wants my sister and me to feel welcome, but she
says that for the first time she appreciates her home as a place
that comforts *her*, instead of one she makes comfortable for
others. It is true that her domestic perspective has shifted, but

perhaps the shift isn't as great as she sometimes thinks. My mother definitely does not keep house with the zeal she once did, but the reasons seem more a reflection of ten-hour workdays outside the home than an enthusiastic heave-ho of domestic responsibility. Only rarely can she sit through a movie without straightening up things in the room, or finishing the dinner dishes, or wrapping a piece of masking tape around three fingers and plucking bits from reupholstered family room chairs. She got tears in her eyes when the gravy was tasteless last Thanksgiving.

"I've let go of some of the cleaning, partly because of Wendell" —her second husband, who considers disorder to be a right. "But I don't like the mess. What I wish now was that we could afford a cleaning lady again." She shifts self-consciously; the idea doesn't sit well.

"Cleaning is sometimes a way to calm down. It's familiar. But sometimes I can't quit. I just keep going and going and going." Her eyes scrunch shut and she pounds the air with her fists. "I lose out on good books, on all kinds of things I define as extras. That's part of the problem. All those things are what I get to do once I've done my jobs."

I study the soft, blond frizziness of her hair, the skin stretched across her cheeks. "But I have much more of a sense of the brevity of existence, and I'm real scared. I want to spend time doing something more worthwhile than cleaning the house."

CONFESSIONS

AND

SEDUCTIONS

Houseguests

JANICE ROSENBERG

I have a confession to make: I used to be uptight about having houseguests. I still am. But let's start at the beginning. No matter who our houseguests were or why they were coming to town, I used to spend weeks making lists of menus, groceries, and chores. I read cookbooks and planned elaborate home-made breakfasts of quiche and yeast coffee cake. The day before my guests' arrival I cleaned the oven, arranged fresh flowers on the dining room table, and hung those small guest towels no one ever uses.

I set aside the last hour for worrying. What would we do between three and five on Saturday afternoon? Did their children eat cheesecake? With creeping anxiety I waited for the doorbell to bring them and their muddy shoes, exploding suitcases, and peculiar allergies into my quiet, calm, well-organized life.

Along with anxiety, I suffered from the nervous buzz of magnified expectations. I looked forward to having visitors. What could be more wonderful than spending a weekend with old friends? Their presence would work a magical change in my ordinary life. We would laugh a lot—at my jokes, of course. We would have the perfect, deep, revealing conversation. They would make me feel cherished as only longtime friends can.

Over the years I housed numerous guests. Some came with their own reasons for tolerating the thin mattress on my sofabed. Nephews borrowed sport jackets for visits to local colleges. Cousins on cross-country motorcycle trips spread the mildewed contents of their backpacks on my bathroom floor. In-laws with clothes in need of ironing attended weddings and bar mitzvahs. College roommates on business trips arranged lunches with old boyfriends. Variously, they stored shoes under the piano, borrowed books they never returned, prowled the kitchen at six A.M. in desperate need of coffee, fed scraps to the dog, and spoiled the children with endless piggyback rides. Dutifully, I wrapped and mailed the hats they left behind and waited for more cooperative visitors.

Yet houseguests who came specifically to spend time with me were equally unsatisfying. They balked at my careful programming, wanted to shop instead of touring the museum exhibit I'd saved for us to share, wrecked my precise timing of the dinner hour by eating Italian beef sandwiches (a Chicago specialty) at four o'clock, yawned just when I thought our most intimate exchanges should get under way. Thoughtful offerings of wine, candy, or homemade chopped liver hardly compensated for such lapses.

Considering my inner clash between obsessive worrying and desperate anticipation, is it any wonder that I concluded every visit with tears and a migraine? Or that visitors left looking perplexed, and, I assume, relieved?

My attitude toward houseguests reached its nadir five years ago when the Fishmans, friends from graduate school, came to Chicago from California for an extra-long Thanksgiving weekend. Since neither their siblings nor their parents had room for overnight guests, I suggested that they stay at our house.

The evening they arrived, the kids went off to reacquaint themselves and we grown-ups reminisced. The next morning I met the Fishmans in the kitchen with fresh rolls and hot coffee. They could have used a press secretary more than a hovering hostess. All their relatives, down to the most distant cousin, wanted to see them. After breakfast they made countless phone calls and held intense councils on what the kids should wear.

This happened each day of their visit. I felt obligated to hang around until they'd left on their day's rounds. Obligated or desperately hopeful? If I'd had any sense, I would have followed my normal daily schedule, gone into my office, and shut the door. Instead I waited for them to leave each morning, feeling bored and put-upon. Which night would they be available to eat the roast beef dinner that I'd planned? When would they have time for a leisurely stroll through our neighborhood? I could not accept the possibility that they never would, at least not on this trip. I envied their relatives for enjoying my friends' company and blamed them for hogging my friends' time while I had nothing but a mess in my guest room.

The day they went back to California, I wasn't sure I ever wanted to see them again. For a long time afterward I concentrated angrily on their lack of consideration. Why hadn't they made time for us? How could they have had the nerve to use our house as a hotel? Only gradually, after a warm (if very late) thank-you note, expressing hopes for less frantic visits here and in California, did I begin to see the truth. The Fishmans had made no effort to disguise the reason for their trip to Chicago. I was the one who'd misconstrued its purpose.

Thinking over similar disappointments, I discovered a common emotional thread: my own need for attention. No guests could ever give enough. Even those who planned specifically to visit with me for a weekend seemed to need space. Could it be that my constant, calculated entertaining—ostensibly done to please my guests, subconsciously done to capture their attention—made everyone uncomfortable? My own determination to go with the flow might solve a dozen problems.

Of course, this observation was easier to make than to apply. I continued to fuss over my brother-in-law's habit of piling his gloves, scarf, pocket contents, and weekend purchases on my narrow front hall table. The Fishmans came again. We had dinner together the first night, and while I didn't expect to see much of them, I did try to tempt them into joining us a second time with grilled New York strip steaks. When my ploy didn't work I reminded myself not to take their busyness personally.

Slowly, being a calm hostess became almost natural. As visitors came and went, I kept all our needs in mind. Taking the plunge, I discovered that guests were happier with bagel-and-cream-cheese breakfasts than with hostesses who nagged them to "get into the kitchen and eat these waffles while they're hot." I recognized that an afternoon on the front porch could be infinitely more satisfying than one spent dragging friends around to movies and exhibits they didn't want to see. When guests came to town with their own agenda, I stuck to my daily rounds and accepted as a bonus whatever free time they had for visiting with me. Little by little, I learned to relax.

This year when my nephew called to say he and his girlfriend would be in town for a wedding, my only preparations were a bigger pot of spaghetti sauce for Friday dinner (in case they happened to arrive on time) and clean sheets on the sofabed. My guests fitted easily into my routine. They made coffee for themselves while I drove my son to a friend's house; they made advance arrangements to borrow the car; they were glad to spend an hour chatting when our schedules met. "Come back anytime," I told them when they left, and I really meant it.

This year when our friends arrived from Cincinnati for New Year's weekend, they found me wearing an apron and slicing potatoes in the kitchen. I let them pile their coats and suitcases anywhere, pointed to the cabinet where I keep the coffee cups, gave them a bag of Oreos to snack on, and didn't worry that I wasn't wearing lipstick or that the music on the stereo might not be to their taste. The only plan I'd made was for that evening—tickets to the theater. I felt confident the four of us would find a dozen things to do over the next few days. And to my delight, we did.

The Split

LAURIE ABRAHAM

Lately, choosing my underwear for the day leaves me cold. I own about thirty pairs, from silky black bikinis to comfortable cotton briefs with red hearts. Before my boyfriend and I separated, I planned my underwear around my day, or my day around my underwear. If Paul and I were going to an art opening, I wore the sexy black ones. He'd appreciate the peach satin pair underneath the Laura Ashley dress my grand-mother sewed. If he was out of town, I'd wear the faded pair. And so on. Now that I'm single, and not inclined to one-night stands, underwear decisions are boring, if not depressing. Underwear was made to be seen; I hate wasting the good things on myself.

Oh, I know I'm supposed to love wearing lacy teddies just for me. Sexy underthings should make me feel special whether a lover gets a look at them or not. They don't. Lingerie only felt good when Paul was sliding his hand over it. But I'm getting off the subject. What I really want to talk about is how my domestic routines have been altered by his absence. With-out realizing it, I've adopted new routines to make up for the loss. And I've abandoned old ones because, for now, certain things, such as interesting underwear, make living alone too lonely.

I'll start with my bed. Last night, I slept with two books, three magazines, my robe and purse, an old blanket, and the phone bill. They got the right side; I got the left. Sticking to my old half of the bed makes me feel more normal. It takes a certain amount of self-confidence and appreciation of freedom to fling your legs across both sides of the bed. When I was living with Paul, I spread out in hotel beds on business trips, valuing those nights to myself. Now, with nothing *but* nights to myself, I've fixed it so that I bump up against things in my bed. If only my robe could mumble and roll over. Though my cluttered bed does serve the purpose I've described, maybe it shows what a slob I've become, too. Without reward, sweep-ing and keeping my clothes off the floor aren't worth the effort. I didn't mind scouring a Saturday away if I could anticipate dinner with Paul. But who cares if dishes pile up in the sink when I'm only cooking for myself? Who cares that the sheets haven't been changed for three weeks if I'm the only one lying on them?

I have not been to the store for more than a month. I would only be going through the motions, buying single woman's food: raspberry yogurt, Lean Cuisine, and turkey loaf. It would spoil, anyway. Sitting down to dinner with Paul was one of my favorite parts of the day; these days, I stay away from my own dining room table. I eat on the run or at work. I've dined on more McDonald's fish sandwiches in the past few weeks than in the past five years.

Of course, I must return home every night, but I haven't been *at* home in weeks. Home was where I had to get up at seven A.M. on Sundays to work in a few hours of writing before I watched the Browns game at noon with Paul. Where I made dinner for the two of us later that day. It's where I came

to recount my evening as a volunteer counselor for rape vic-
tims. Where someone would bring me tea and sit next to me
on the couch. Where I had a dance partner when the Euryth-
mics, or in a different mood, Cat Stevens, sang on the radio.
Solace, companionship, an occasional dance: these things I
expect from home. But single people can't get these things at
home.

It seems that I am refusing to care for my home because I do
not feel like I have one any more. When women of my
mother's generation divorced (and after seven years with Paul,
I feel divorced), I don't think they were as likely to throw out
their domestic responsibilities with their husbands. They still
felt as if they had a home; they may not have had a man
around, but more often than not they had children filling their
rooms, chattering, laughing, whining. They still had the people that make a home a home. It embarrasses me how much I
depend on a man—or children, for that matter—to give me a
sense of home. Growing up, I imagined I would remain single,
that I would be content spending evenings alone in my apartment. The single woman I imagined was self-assured, tough-
minded; she had lots of close woman friends. When I got
older, she began to scorn me because I had never lived alone. I
would occasionally consider striking out on my own, living
apart from Paul. It would be a good experience; I'd be stronger
for it, I would tell myself. That was before Paul asked me to
move out.

I want to feel better, to put some order back into my life,
but I'm not ready. Some of my friends are on the road to
recovery—this has been the season for severing; all my closest friends have left boyfriends, or have been left, in the last
six months—and I can see that they're feeling more comfortable on their own when I walk through their front doors. Barb
has a new double bed, which she bought a couple of months
after her lover left for San Francisco. She also got sheets he
would have hated: white cotton with a thin blue-purple pin-
stripe. Lisa hid pictures of Roger in the basement and asked to

borrow my old bedspread; the paisley one brought back too many memories. Now she's far enough away from the ordeal to switch back to paisley because *she* likes it. After Peter decided he wanted to date other women, Janice framed an Ansel Adams print of San Francisco Bay that had been leaning against her wall for a year. And she says she's going to buy a kitchen clock, something that would have seemed too practical, too domestic, too trivial while she was dating Peter.

One day, I, too, will give my home a little respect. It will be my place, not what's left of me and Paul. My recovery is plodding; I lived with Paul off and on from the time I was twenty. I have managed to throw away some of his mismatched socks. I returned two of his sweaters and stashed his pictures in the bottom of a drawer. I will take back my home, though I confess that I probably always will feel most *at* home sharing my space, my underwear, with someone. But at my best moments I'm excited that I've not found a home yet; adventures lie ahead. When I was getting ready for work the other day, I came across a high-cut pair of underpants I bought to please Paul only days before our farewell. I was surprised that they did not depress me. Someone else will appreciate them one day, I thought to myself. I started to put them back in the drawer. Then I put them on.

Dream Houses

NANCY EBERLE

The tall, flame-colored lilies are in bloom now, along with the flat round heads of yarrow and the willowy delphiniums. So why am I sitting in this high-rise in the city, instead of out in the country where I belong?

The old farmhouse is finished now—so tight and snug that in winter we can let the embers from the previous night's fire die and let the sun heat the house until the afternoon shadows turn blue on the snow. The road is now a proper road, and all but the last bit of fencing is done. So why am I looking not at lilies and delphiniums, but on the dull grass of the park below?

The move back to the city was harder in many ways than the move away from it, for I grew to love that garden, and the mulberry tree in the middle of it, and the hills beyond it and the sky above it with an abiding love I never came close to having for anything in the city. I know exactly where on the horizon the sun rises and where it sets at this time of year and where to look for the wren when I hear her singing through the bedroom window. I can recognize the individual bleats of each of fifty sheep when they return to the barnyard for water. So why, to take up my refrain, am I here instead of there?

I wish I knew the answer. Like my mother before me, who moved us thirteen times in half as many years and whom I forgave only in death, perhaps I am afflicted with a vision of The One Best Place. Her favorite Biblical quotation was "In my father's house are many mansions," in which I believe she took both justification for her many moves and comfort when they went wrong.

The idea of One Best Place made us leave the city in the first place, when more reasonable folk might have relaxed into the privileged duality of a summer home. We saw the farm, we fell in love with it, we bought it—and then we sold everything else and sallied forth, liked two innocents on their way to high adventure. Our journey had a more than passing similarity to *Mosquito Coast*.

We left, five years later, after a little soul-searching. The hard part had overwhelmed the fun part—I suppose it came down to that, although perhaps I am being too demanding. Certainly there were plenty of more solid reasons. To support us, my husband, Dick, had to work in the city, 150 miles distant. This meant that we lived separate lives except on weekends and that I was alone with a young child in isolated (and in winter downright hazardous) circumstances. Meanwhile, I had come to miss the presence of colleagues—people whose work interests were the same as my own. Our family had changed, too. We arrived on the farm a party of five: ourselves, two sons in their last years of high school, and a three-year-old daughter. When we left, the boys had already preceded us and were in their first years of college. Their leaving diminished the whole experience in untold ways, for we had purchased the dream not only of adventure but of a *Little House on the Prairie* vision of family life as well. But beyond all this, or perhaps before it, was the simple fact that it had stopped being fun. We were restless. And so we moved. We kept the farm though, our love for it strangely undiminished for its having finally become a weekend home. Perhaps absence does make the heart grow fonder.

If our tale is unusual in the extremity of the choices we made (and in the economic freedom we had to make them), I think that certain elements of it are nonetheless universal. I am talking about dreams and how central a role the place where we live plays in them. (I suppose there must be people whose dreams are totally devoid of habitat, but I cannot imagine it, myself.) I think we get ourselves into a lot of trouble this way. The most obvious example is falling in love with a lifestyle completely foreign to our nature. It happens all the time. We visit the starkly contemporary home of a new friend. How spacious, we think. How serene. How very beautiful. How different our lives would be if only we lived in such a place. We return to our previously beloved house and find—a chotchke-laden mess. How awful, we think. How did we ever make such an error? But in truth we haven't made an error: we are about to make one, in thinking that we could be the masters of that contemporary house without undergoing lobotomies first.

It's a costly business, whether we act on our dreams or not. It's as costly to pine for the wrong thing as it is to have it. On the other hand, I wouldn't want to live without dreams. The trick, I guess, is to have dreams that are consonant with who you are.

I wonder if my mother, when she was making all those moves, had a dream after all, or whether she was simply acting upon impulse born out of desperation. I know a few of the facts. Her job as a reporter was poorly paid and she was desperate for money, having been widowed and left with a small child, without any insurance and certainly without money for day care, which didn't even exist then anyway. I know, too, that it was wartime and apartments were hard to come by. I know this because she would bring home—wherever home was—families whose eviction she was writing about for the newspaper. No matter that we barely had room for ourselves; we certainly had enough to share with someone whose circumstances were even worse than our own. But these few facts do not go far in explaining the constant succession of apartments and hotels and rooming houses in which I spent my childhood years. I think probably my mother was caught in a cycle that went like this: She would quit her job on the newspaper to take a job in public relations, which offered more money (never mind that it also offered no security whatever). In the euphoria and hope of that advancement, she would move into a better apartment down the street, which perhaps cost a little too much but which would be paid for by the new accounts she surely would get. When the new accounts failed to materialize or the old one responsible for her having been hired fell apart, she would be forced to give up the apartment and move somewhere less expensive. And then the cycle would repeat itself. Back to the paper, catch up on the debts, find a better place to live. Find a better job, lose it, find a cheaper place to live.

So the facts suggest that our constant moving was part exigency and park fecklessness, but I think I can detect the work of dreams as well. All this is nothing more than to say that another woman might have been content to stay in the boardinghouse or the third floor walk-up where fate had deposited her.

For years I resented all those moves—or rather, I resented the abrupt severance of relationships that they caused. Did I ever finish out the year in the same school where I started? I don't think so. I went through early adulthood believing that I wanted nothing more than to stay in one place and to give my children when they arrived, the security that had been denied me. But now I wonder if that's true. Certainly it was a wretched way to grow up for the simple reason of chronic, unremitting loneliness. But what it left in me may not have been the longing to stay in one place after all, but rather a restlessness and enjoyment of change for its own sake.

I never drive down a leafy city street with three-story brick houses set back from the curb without dreaming about moving into one of them. I never drive my daughter forty-five minutes to her suburban music lesson without wondering if the suburbs aren't the ultimate solution after all. And I never drive to the farm for a weekend without yearning for the life that late I led, or wander among the lilies without wondering what I am doing sitting here, a hostage in a high-rise, dreaming dreams.

It seems a terrible waste to invest so much of our life's energy and time in moving about. I look with distaste upon women who redecorate annually—have they nothing more significant to do with their lives? But changing houses is different. When you change houses you're trying on a life. That's what it's all about, really. I don't know whether that makes it more acceptable or not. But I know you'd better know who you are—or be content to spend that time and energy finding out.

The Mess

MARY BETH DANIELSON

Don't touch. Please, please pick up the clutter in your room. Take your feet off the sofa. Wash your hands. I'm telling you for the last time to set the table. No TV until you've emptied the dishwasher. Don't touch.

This litany of exasperation is so familiar because we seem to spend our whole lives at one end or the other of it. We escape the tyranny of our mother's good furniture only to lust after our own. At the same time, in total foolhardiness, we attempt to raise children. Where are our minds?

Kids are messy. Kids are dirty. Kids pursue comfort at the expense of your house. Concepts like order and responsibility fly over their heads like geese flying north in the spring. Beauty is something they pursue with mascara and purple eyeshadow.

We end up in twenty-year wars with our children over the way our houses look. Children simply don't care. What they ask of life is something interesting to do for a while and then a place to sprawl.

The thing is, I can understand being a kid. I remember when the whole world, especially my parents' ordinary living room, seemed inviting. I played hide-and-seek behind chairs. I'd invent dramas for the china figurines. My brother and I built long winding roads out of books, on which we drove his model cars.

I think of those times as I watch Lilly hard at play now. She pushes her doll buggy from room to room. She misses corners, smashes into chairs, makes small dents in the wall. She's been learning to color for a year, and she still wanders off the paper, leaving faint red and purple streaks on the coffee table. She blithely digs, explores, and investigates our house and yard. I know that she needs to play in a familiar place, just as I did when I was the kid in my parents' home. This is, after all, her home. The price for this security is that I often feel like I'm on bivouac in a kindergarten.

So how do we live with the chaos, the ordinary mess generated by the children who live with us? The answer has to be: by remembering, by forgiving, and by drawing the line.

There is a line between respecting your child and letting your child rule the roost. Given the chance, any kid worth his salt will swerve back and forth over that line like a drunken sailor on leave in Singapore. So we decide what the bottom line is and demand that our kids make their beds in the morning or pick up their toys at night.

But it is also worth our while to imagine what it feels like to be the children in our homes. Think of a kid, flat on her back on your carpeted floor, legs hooked up and over the cushions of the sofa. Her head is turned slightly toward the glow of after-school television as her hand dips effortlessly into a bag of potato chips. Imagine how good that must feel at four o'clock in the afternoon.

We confuse beauty and serenity. We are used to thinking of beauty as rich furnishings, cleverly arranged, perfectly clean and neat. This beauty comes with the unspoken promise that if you spend all your time and money and energy attaining it, then you will have serenity also.

I am discovering that I can—and probably will—live with wall-to-wall toys, muddy floors, and cracker crumbs in my bed for the next ten years, because that's the milieu of happy kids, and happy kids create a noisy, messy serenity. When my soul is shrinking at the never-ending eyesore, I try to remember that this is a home where four people live and that two of them are children. My husband and I have a right to some order, and when we have time, we clean down to it. But children also have a right to an open-hearted environment. It's their house, too.

Upstairs

CARROLL STONER

We lived on the third floor. Once, at a party on the first floor, our second-floor neighbor told me, as she laughed, that she could hear "everything" that went on in our bedroom, since it was right above their own. I was shocked by her candor, but even more outraged at the thought that she had such intimate knowledge about my marriage. In fact, I was so irritated by her claim, delivered with an elbow in my ribs and a sidelong glance, that I ran upstairs to my apartment. Like those mothers who find superhuman strength and lift cars off their children, I singlehandedly moved our bed and stuffed a combination of bathroom rugs and towels under its supports. I told my son to jump on it until I called on the phone to tell him to stop, ran down to the second-floor apartment where the neighbors' daughter let me in, and listened until I was reassured that our bed was now soundless. Not a creak.

I returned to the party, took my neighbor aside, and told her she'd never hear anything from my bedroom again. I would not tell her why, which drove her crazy. I smiled when I told her. But I was not laughing about it, either then or now.

Such are the vicissitudes of apartment living—the things you reveal about yourselves. And my, what you can learn about your neighbors!

The last apartment we lived in was in a vintage building with just thirty families—small enough so that everyone felt compelled to stop and chat when we met in the elevator or lobby. Then, I thought it was fine. Now that I've moved to an apartment in a smaller building, I realize how invasive it was.

The lobby itself finally got to me. When we moved into the building, the lobby was unbelievably ugly, decorated one taste level above orange shag carpeting. A committee had been formed to redecorate it, and soon it looked attractive, low-key, even a bit elegant. But then it became de rigueur to discuss the lobby every time you met someone there. "Wasn't it awful? All that money for (take your pick) the antique table, the leather sofas, the terrible lamps. . . ." Two factions arose, one that loved and defended it, another attacking those who felt neutral or defensive.

We were part of a subgroup that neither loved nor hated it—we're talking about a lobby here—but supported those who had made the decisions. Finally, I made a promise not to utter one more word about it. The next time I ran into the leader of the "hate-the-lobby" group, I told her of my decision and suggested she follow suit, making it clear, I thought, that the lobby was a dead issue. Being sucked into such a foolish controversy is one of the dangers of cooperative living, which is what apartment living is all about.

I never learned the names of the people who lived below us in that building, and I was glad I hadn't when the woman broke all rules of protocol by asking me what our children did upstairs all afternoon, run from one end of the apartment to the other? In a concrete building where I'd never heard so much as a footfall from my own upstairs neighbors, and at a time when my five-year-old wasn't even home most after-noons? I was mute. Her husband apologized instantly, but it was too late. I never stopped wondering what in the hell she meant and was relieved each year when they went to Florida in October and stayed until April.

I knew next to nothing about the semiretired couple who lived above us. I did know, for example, that their maid used to spend hours every day vacuuming their rugs until I would begin to fear for her sanity. (This period was during a time when I worked out of my home and, fearing for my own sanity, may have expressed my fear in worry about others' well-being.) She spent most of every morning running the vacuum back and forth, back and forth until I thought she must have fallen under the hypnotic spell of a Hoover upright that was not even her own.

A friend tells how she knew her upstairs neighbors made love in the middle of the night, and says that once she knew, she could picture them in the bed, him plopped on top of her (the image came from her belief that not many women would choose that time for lovemaking). After that, she didn't want to know them, and never did learn even so much as what they did for a living.

We learn everything related to plumbing and intimacy about our neighbors. When they flush their toilets early in the morning, it reminds us that at the age of thirty or so, we can no longer sleep through the night with a full bladder. We know when they take showers and baths and what time their children go to bed by the sound of the various footfalls. We know what time they all get up in the morning. When we live in apartments with thin walls, we learn about neighbors' musical tastes, how and when they fight, how and when they make up, and how they get along with their children.

If they are a sweet family, as our present upstairs neighbors are, no one minds. Their three-year-old never walks, but runs. She is one of those beautiful, tiny children who make you smile, so reminiscent are they of some perfect vision of childhood. Hearing her run evokes the same, warm feelings that seeing her does.

But I'll never forget living upstairs over a terrible, usually silent family and hearing the father beat his seven- or eight-year-old son. The father and son shared a furtive quality and too-short pale brown hair. Neither of them could quite hold his head up and look you straight in the eye, and that look is what I envision when I read about child abuse—a kind of leashed anger at powerlessness that can only be let out in the privacy of a basement apartment. It was my first apartment in New York and I can still remember the shock, my own tears, and finally leaving so I didn't have to listen. I forgive myself for not calling the police only by remembering that I was not yet filled with the confidence that bequeathes righteous indignation.

We've had a few less-than-stellar moments of our own in the privacy of our home, though they never quite pushed us to physical violence. Fighting (arguing, that is) with your husband is tricky when you live in an apartment. Does such restraint help or hurt marriages? Who knows? The fact that the two most crowded island kingdoms on earth, England and Japan, are inhabited by the most restrained people is no accident. The closer we live to one another, the higher the invisible walls we build.

When I was young, I didn't mind thin walls. As I've matured, my walls have thickened. Still, I prefer city living, partly because it comes without the isolation of single-family home life, but also because of the stimulation that comes from rubbing shoulders with friends and strangers. There is a delicate balance between the need to live with strangers and shops and busy streets nearby, and the need to know intimate things about others and reveal as much about ourselves. Living upstairs is part of the bargain.

I have chosen life in a city apartment over life in a suburban house. Having my work, our children's schools, and our home within a few minutes of one another has a lot to do with the decision. Life in a house seems impossible, somehow out of the question. It has something to do with a house and yard's incessant demands for upkeep and its public expression of who you are.

I grew up in a single-family home, standing alone in its small yard, surrounded by flowers and a tidy lawn. Years after my mother died and we moved, I drove by it and was surprised by how angry I felt about the now messy, overgrown yard. My mother's flower beds, laboriously planted and lovingly cared for, were dead and gone. Didn't the people know how plain, how unloved, the house looked?

But wouldn't I be just like them? Without the courage to be one of those suburban cranks who cements over his front yard or lets it all go to hell, I would forever be ambivalent about declaring just how much I did (or didn't) care about the external appearance of our home.

And so I have chosen to let neighbors know other, probably far more intimate things about us.

Dishwashers

JANICE ROSENBERG

Until recently, my husband had nothing to do with the dishwasher. I loaded it, turned it on at bedtime, and emptied it each afternoon when I went into the kitchen to start dinner. In the morning, rather than open the dishwasher and take a clean soup spoon out of the silverware basket, my husband would use a teaspoon for his Cheerios. If no spoons remained in the drawer, he ate a bagel. And seethed.

One morning, after drinking his orange juice out of an

empty cruet, he broke down and asked why I couldn't change my schedule and unload the dishwasher before breakfast. He said dirty dishes left in the sink until four P.M. repelled him. I said my job as housekeeper began at four o'clock. Rather than go into the ideological arguments that ensued I will only say that, in a burst of sharing, he took on the task himself.

Many domestic spats revolve around the dishwasher—who should load/unload, when is it too full/too empty, and, most important, what happens when there are no dishes left in the cupboard. For some people the frustration and postponed gratification caused by having to wash a dish before eating a newly created Dagwood sandwich is simply too great. For others, running a partly loaded machine undermines their deepest beliefs in efficiency. The second date is not too soon to begin negotiations on these subjects.

Although my sister-in-law and I disagree on basic loading methods—she laughs in the face of order, I follow patterns as rigid as Robert's Rules—we both know the value of getting in every possible plate. At a recent holiday dinner, she and I amused my mother-in-law (her mother) with our stacking feats. As if watching a juggler balance just one more cup and saucer atop his head, she applauded each "impossible" addition to the loaded racks. We asked her why she was so willing to wash so much by hand. She acted as if her washer were a servant whom she did not want to burden. "I don't want to wear it out," she said.

This brings up another bone of contention: scraping. How much is enough? This can be determined to a reasonable degree of satisfaction by an equation balancing age of dishwasher, length of time dishes will sit prior to running of dishwasher, and food type. For example, home economists have shown beyond a doubt that bran flakes left in a breakfast bowl will not be removed by a ten P.M. washing in a ten-year-old machine. On the other hand, a new machine will remove coffee stains from breakfast mugs left standing over week-long vacations. In middle age, a machine can usually be trusted to dissolve the remains of ice cream sundaes.

Still, like everything else, dishwashing is a question of personal preference. My neighbor simply cannot stand to have a machine half full of dirty dishes marring her otherwise perfectly spotless kitchen, even if no one can see inside. Since she is an efficient businesswoman, she probably applies the same principles to her briefcase. Others expect the machine to do the work of a garbage disposal. This expectation can lead to circumstances too horrible to envision: breakdown and the repairman's visit.

Once my husband stopped treating the dishwasher like a leper, he began loading as well as unloading. But when our sons get into the act, they ignore the carefully thought-out methods we use and we enter a double-bind situation. Of course we want our kids to do more than leave their sticky plates beside the sink, but do we want them interfering with our ultrarefined arrangements?

When I've stood over the machine setting each plate in the same direction, sliding bowls into special corners, puzzling out a position for the gravy boat, hooking each glass over its own plastic coated pin, do I want my twelve-year-old to throw off the balance with a frying pan I never would put into the washer in the first place? (Well, yes, if I want him to master household chores. But that's another story.) Meditating at the upper rack, waiting for revelation on the perfect location for the pasta bowl, am I pleased to have a teenage hand dip in from out of bounds and drop a chocolate-milk glass just anywhere? Chocolate-milk dregs drip over the dinner plates, onto the open washer door, and into the detergent dispenser. But how can I complain when it's taken my kids years to realize that plates aren't moved from table to sink by poltergeists?

Sure, in the dark ages people got along without dishwashers. Even now some hardy souls insist that shared hand washing and drying provide rare conversation time in busy lives. The rest of us are dishwasher-dependent. And like most household appliances, dishwashers time their breakdowns for the worst possible moments.

One year on the day before a Passover Seder to which my mother had invited twenty people, she received a bushel of Florida oranges from a thoughtful friend. Being an efficient housekeeper, she dug out her Mixmaster's juicing attachment and got to work. All those orange rinds proved too much for her disposal. How was she to know that the disposal and dishwasher shared a drain? She spent the night baling orange pulp from the bottom of her dishwasher, called a repairman, and in the meantime washed the Seder dishes in the bathtub.

When a man I know was asked as part of a party game to name the two most valuable inventions of the twentieth century, he proclaimed, "The internal combustion engine and the micro chip." His wife looked at him as if he had just landed from another planet. When her turn came she did not hesitate. "The tampon and the dishwasher," she said. The men laughed, but the women knew just what she was talking about.

Table Settings

NANCY EBERLE

If I had a million dollars, I'd spend the first $5,000 on china. I'd buy the bowls that look like cantaloupes and the tureen that looks like a rabbit and the plates that look like asparagus. I'd have different dishes for every occasion: the cow that pours milk for the children's breakfast; terra-cotta bowls with blazed interiors for chili on a winter's night; antique blue-and-white flow ware for chocolate cake on a Sunday afternoon.

Nor is china the end of it. I'd buy masses of cyclamens for Valentine's Day and put nosegays of violets on rose-colored napkins for a springtime luncheon. I'd buy every fabric I ever loved—chintz and madras and deep purple cotton—and stacks and stacks of napkins in every hue from indigo to bittersweet.

Of all the creative possibilities inherent in domestic life, there's none that sings to me more than the simple act of setting the table. Rooms take time to decorate, mistakes in hanging pictures leave marks, painting is boring after you've done the first wall. But setting the table encourages daring, forgives mistakes, and gives immediate gratification.

When I was growing up, it was my privilege as the oldest grandchild to set the table for Thanksgiving dinner. If I close my eyes, I can still feel the weight and slippery coolness of the heavy damask cloth as I carried it, solemn as any acolyte, to the mahogany table, where my grandfather had put in the extra leaves and spread the faded brown table pad. When I lifted the lid of the silver chest in the middle drawer of the big buffet, mysterious objects gleamed against the crushed blue velvet lining ("What's that, Grandma?" "That's a pickle fork, toots.") This was clearly the stuff of high ceremony.

I grew up, settled down, got a job, and with my very first paycheck, made a down payment on a set of stainless steel flatware. By the time I was engaged three years later, my taste had returned to sterling, and I picked a pattern so pricey that my fiancé's mother kept it a secret from her friends, who were probably the only ones able to afford it. The result: one knife, two teaspoons, and goodbye elegance.

Today my taste is neither stainless nor sterling. What I crave is variety—as many kinds of china as Imelda Marcos has shoes. I moon over the tableaux in the china department the way some people covet model rooms. But I have neither the cash, the space, nor the conscience to indulge my fantasies, so what I have is something else: basic black. Black? Yes, black: a mottled pattern of shiny and matte black, as sophisticated as a panther (which everyone knows is a leopard with black spots), as earthy as the not-quite-perfect circles of its handthrown rims. Against it the food gleams with the intensity of paint on an artist's palette: the red of pimiento, the intense green of broccoli, the gold of squash, the parchment color of brown rice. What is innocuous on white is audacious on black.

I still moon over majolica, but I no longer have the hunger to possess that is more like lust than love. Somewhere along the way I have lost the acquisitive instinct. What remains is something more benign: the occasional child's play of "If I had a million dollars . . ." And so each evening I set my table with panther plates. And with pleasure.

The Country Kitchen

CARROLL STONER

She had a country kitchen once. It was the kitchen of her dreams.

Three weeks after the carpenter sanded the last plane on the open, doorless pine shelves and she placed the gleaming, clear-glass canisters in line, she had her first tiny nagging doubt. It came when she reached for the pasta and felt the gritty, slightly greasy canister jar slip through her grip. It didn't break because she clutched at it with both hands and avoided dropping it on her new terra-cotta floor, which was fortunate since everything that dropped onto the hard, cool tile broke instantly. A week or so later she looked at the dishes on the open shelf that ran from window to inner wall and saw how disorder was creeping into the neatly stacked piles of plates and cups. Where did that extra, unmatched cup come from? And the two odd glasses?

And so it went, nagging doubt atop irritating worry; the compulsion to keep her showplace clean mixed with the desire to feel she was not tied to the kitchen. After two years had passed, she finally admitted what had grown from small doubt into full-fledged certainty: Her country kitchen was a failure.

During that time she had plenty of opportunities to observe the intricate pattern of how things worked in her house. Keeping the kitchen tidy meant that she spent extra time there, for one thing, but that wasn't so bad, since she believed the kitchen was the heart of her house. So for a while the constant tidying didn't even feel like work. And yes, it was nice to use one movement getting a spice jar from the basket atop the ceramic tile island without having to stop, open a cabinet door, and fumble around a dark shelf for the right jar. But the small jars and the large handsome basket that held them soon felt as gritty and oily to the touch as the canisters.

She had time to think about it as she sat, elbows propped atop the hand-painted tiles of the center island, which was about as cold as a tabletop could be. Here she had been in the habit of sitting and reading the morning paper as she sipped coffee from her favorite mug (the one her stepdaughter made at camp that didn't match any of the others on the shelf). Now, she read and reflected on what looked like dirt in the grout that separated the handsome flowered tiles from one another.

As she looked around her, she knew she should feel fortunate. In urban and suburban homes across America, women dreamed about kitchens designed to look as though they were moved in one piece from French and Italian and Portuguese villas. But slowly the awakening came, and with it the understanding that the reason her kitchen didn't work was because her life was about as different from that of a chatelaine of a country chateau as country is from city.

The open kitchen had some wonderful qualities. It expressed her style—sort of—and people oohed and aahed when they entered. The hanging bouquets of peppers and garlic and the bay-leaf wreath were as convenient as the cookie jar. The orderly row of canisters was beautiful. Like oversized mason jars, they looked best when filled with all the whole grains and rice and pastas that advertise you've come a long way from macaroni and cheese.

But the work! Keeping those jars shiny and free of fingerprints, lining up the two sizes of glasses three deep and four across, with the three sizes of plates stacked alongside the dozen cups in identical size and shape . . . This lifestyle was not for someone who couldn't resist a box of unmatched relish dishes and platters at a country auction. It was all wrong for the woman who wanted to walk into a kitchen at the last minute and toss a meal together in an atmosphere that might or might not be perfect order behind the closed cabinet doors.

After a few months she made the sensible decision that the jars didn't have to be emptied and washed just because they were dirty. She continued to buy glasses by the dozen and put away anything that disturbed the symmetry of the sets, and she made a policy of moving all the extra stuff that crept onto the shelves into below-the-counter cabinets. She begrudged the time she spent crouching and peering into the nether regions that now held her kitchen's odds and ends, those pieces not pretty enough, or not part of matched sets, and thus not displayed on the open shelves.

Finally, though she couldn't quite have doors reinstalled on the open cabinets or replace the open shelves with conventional cupboards, she did put her spices away and take her appliances out from down under. She left up her bay-leaf wreath and rationalized that although the leaves had lost much of their fragrance and felt slightly greasy, she'd use two for the flavor once bestowed by one, and the grime would cook off in the process.

Ten years later, the wreath still hangs on her kitchen wall, providing a lifetime supply of bay leaves and a reminder of a kitchen in the past.

Living Together

JANICE ROSENBERG

I brought home the newspaper. He stopped for a loaf of rye bread. I defrosted the mixed vegetables. He grilled the lamb chops in the countertop broiler. We ate dinner at the big table in his parents' dinette, sometimes scantily dressed because of the heat. I did the dishes. He swept the floor and carried the bag of garbage out to the incinerator. Neither of us considered the condition of the appliances or the stock in the cupboards. We were only playing house.

His mother had left plenty of food when she and his father went for a month in the Berkshires. She told him he should sleep in their room because of the air conditioning. Rather than bothering to change the sheets, he should simply switch from one of the pushed together twin beds to the other after a week. The "girl," as she called her housecleaning person, would come once in the middle of the month. His mother didn't tell him not to worry about dust or bathroom grime; there wasn't a chance in the world that he would.

She also didn't tell him what to do about his girlfriend— namely, me. But could his mother have been so naïve as to think I wouldn't move in? Both of us were twenty years old that summer. I was going to summer school while he worked at his college library. I was staying in the dorm, in a single room. No one was around to question my absence. Sign-out sheets and curfews had been dispensed with for the summer.

With his parents safely a hundred miles away, mine an even safer thousand, I moved into the apartment on a day-to-day basis. Late afternoons I would take an uptown train and meet him at the building. If his mother was naïve, the doorman certainly was not. We could practically see him wink as we passed, even when we passed separately five minutes apart.

It was nineteen sixty-six. Some unmarried couples lived together openly, but we were too conventional, too dependent on our parents' good will and financial support. We'd been dating for two years by then. Did anyone really believe that we weren't sleeping together? But back then good children maintained a pretense of purity. Our parents warned us in vague terms about the usual pitfalls of sexual activity. All the same, we believed, they preferred to think of us as innocent. And so we protected them from the truth—that we were growing up.

For those four weeks we lived in his parent's apartment where he had lived all through college, where he had been brought home from the hospital as an infant. The doormen remembered him sitting in his stroller, waiting for the day camp bus, dressed for his bar mitzvah, going off on his first date. Even in that large New York apartment house, most of the neighbors knew him.

One neighbor owned a smooth-haired fox terrier and walked him what seemed like at least a dozen times a day. When we went out for an evening stroll or walked back late from the subway station at Seventy-ninth Street, we were especially careful to keep a lookout for the dog lady. His mother called her a gossip. Assuming she would snitch on us, we hid in stores or crossed the street when we saw her coming. Our silly ostrich act brought no repercussions. She was either truly oblivious or more tactful than we thought.

We slept soundly and awoke every morning to the radio. The disk jockey—one of the shouting variety—reported that the "L.I.E. was L.O.L." That meant he wished commuters on the Long Island Expressway lots of luck. He played the latest tunes, cuts from the Beatles' Rubber Soul album and "Hot Town Summer in the City," appropriately sung by the Lovin' Spoonful. We made love and danced naked, then took deep breaths of air-conditioned air and stepped through the bedroom's double doors into the thick, humid July air that swamped the remainder of the apartment.

Those four weeks we kept up our pretense of sneaking around, more as a joke than out of any real fear of being caught. We left the building separately and met at a nearby coffee shop for breakfast. I felt incredibly sophisticated unfolding my section of the *New York Times* (a newspaper that bored me silly) while seated at the counter of this neighborhood greasy spoon. I drank coffee and smeared grape jelly on my buttered toast. At the corner we kissed goodbye. He took the train uptown while I headed down.

When I was among anonymous grown-ups—waiting in the subway station, standing in the crowded train, walking from Sheridan Square through the already hot day—I kept my head up, swung my arms. As much as I enjoyed playing house with him, I liked knowing that I was on my own until evening. I relished the security of having someone waiting for me at the end of the day, but in the meantime, I would mostly do as I pleased.

Before class I stopped at the dorm to change clothes and pick up my books. I was taking Spanish and music—easy, entertaining subjects. After class I went to the park and ate lunch, a sandwich or a buttered roll and a container of cottage cheese. I spent the afternoon in my room, studying, then watching Art Linkletter's "House Party" on my ancient TV. During commercials I read *The Brothers Karamazov*. When the show ended, I listened to symphonies by Brahms and César Franck while I flipped through my homemade Spanish flash cards.

Did I really love that small, compact single dorm room, or does it only seem special in retrospect? I cannot say for sure. Instead I find the answer implicit in my visceral reactions.

Thinking back evokes only pleasurable sensations; conjuring up those long-ago surroundings revives a deep feeling of satisfaction. That summer I took comfort in the corner captain's bed, in the look of my possessions neatly arranged on the desk, and in the open closet: my shoes in pairs, my books in rows. In that room I could replenish my inner life, reading, dreaming, thinking, playing one movement of a concerto over and over, watching inane television shows without drawing criticism of any kind.

It took me years to find that kind of sanctuary within the framework of our married life, to realize my right to have some space and to recognize my need for it. Once married, I lost touch with the value of making my own private nest. Back then, by chance and instinct, I understood.

That summer, late in the afternoon, I would venture out into the steamy day. Sometimes I chose to walk a good distance north before heading into the subway, exercising my body and my freedom. In the lobby of his building I greeted the doorman. I let myself into the apartment, the silence broken only by the grandfather clock chiming the half-hour. On the tenth floor a warm but pleasant breeze rattled the Venetian blinds and billowed the kitchen curtains.

Having arrived first, I sprawled in an armchair, looking at the cartoons in his father's collection of *New Yorkers*. It never occurred to me to make the beds or start our dinner before he arrived. That job would come later, when we were married. For now we were only playing house.

Dressing Husbands

CARROLL STONER

There is a dirty little secret of married life that women are hesitant to confess. We tell only our best friends, and that's only when our annoyance level overrides our need for discretion. Between occasional confidences, we're too busy to pay much attention to this little dilemma, but too proud to let it go.

The problem: We dress our husbands.

I don't mean we tell them upsy-daisy and bend their arms into shirts. I mean we insist on telling them what to wear for what occasion, and sometimes why. This work is time-consuming, because instead of appreciating our attention to their details, they often argue with our advice, saying things like "Okay, I'll change, but I'm going to be way overdressed."

We persevere, and for good reasons, the main one being that we don't trust them to dress themselves. It comes to something simple: We're afraid their taste in clothes will embarrass us.

When I told an old friend I'd bought my husband cute matching undershirts and underpants in bright colors, she warned me about their potential for problems. She had bought the same Calvin Kleins for her husband but had had to throw out the T-shirts. Her husband had started wearing them as shirts on weekends.

"I hated having to get rid of them," she said, laughing sheepishly because of the combination of snobbery and frugal-ity it revealed, "but I didn't want him hanging around the house looking like Elmer Fudd, in his overwashed, slightly too-small, teal-blue T-shirt."

In truth our task is usually aimed more at public than private clothes. Most women admit to occasionally forcing their husbands to change before they go out at night because they are dressed wrong. The men may grump and get mad, but knowing we know what we're talking about, they change.

My own husband, blessed with impeccable taste in business suits, has been known to wake me up at 5:30 A.M. to get my approval on a tie-and-shirt combination. I almost always give my imprimatur, but when I don't, he sometimes stands alongside our bed and defends his choice. It's one thing to be awakened for a yes or no choice. It's another to have to defend why a tie with a blue in it that looks purple does not go with a blue shirt and navy blue suit, or why a small-scale paisley tie doesn't always go with a wide-striped shirt of the same color but is perfect with a narrow-striped shirt of another shade.

Think of the chaos if they had, as we do, all the options in the world in terms of mixing and matching a daily outfit. Think of the time it would take us not only to buy the clothes but to help them mix and match as well. Thank God for dark suits and black tie. God help us if the dress code disappears.

All this, of course, is why men wear uniforms.

Those years of reading *Seventeen*, then *Mademoiselle* and *Glamour*, and then on to the serious big-time fashion mags, pay off. We know about clothes the way men know about cars or baseball or computers. In the long run, this knowledge is probably a bad bargain. In theory I'd rather know the difference between the Jaguar XJS and the XJ than between voile and moiré.

But our knowledge of men's clothing is superficial. Not one of the women I questioned for this piece knew the difference between a Windsor and a Gordian knot, and nobody knew anything about the correct length of a man's suit coat or sport jacket.

"Should his ass hang out a little bit?" asked one seriously.

"Only if it's cute," said another as everyone laughed.

"My husband is always asking me if his tie is too short," said a doctor's wife, married sixteen years, "and I still don't know what to tell him. Do ties come in different lengths?"

Another woman offered the helpful thought that perhaps tall men need longer ties.

And did these women know anything about "dressing right" and "dressing left"?

"What's that?" asked the hip twenty-three-year-old at the same time as the thirty-seven-year-old.

It has to do with having pants tailored with room for a man's scrotum, on one or the other side of the pants' crotch seams.

"Are you kidding? Is that a joke?" they asked as the room exploded in laughter.

Into this free-for-all atmosphere, one of the women told a story making the point that if we know little about men's clothes, they know (as we already knew) even less.

While being measured for suit pants, a young man was asked by the tailor, in the tailor's most polite voice, which side he wore his "gentlemen's" on. Just as politely, the young man asked him to repeat the question.

When the tailor repeated it and the young man still didn't get it, the hard-pressed tailor shouted impatiently, "Your balls, kid, your balls."

I once had a boss who came to town months before his wife joined him. He was the editor of a major metropolitan daily newspaper and he wore white socks and a sport jacket that stopped inches above his wrists until the day his wife arrived. She must have thrown away his too-small, medium-blue sport coat (too bright to be basic and too light to be right) and all those dumb white socks, because within a week he was in dark suits. They may not have been elegant, but they weren't embarrassing. (As I got to know him and saw how often we were going to disagree, I realized that dressing badly was the least of my worries.)

A friend tells how her husband, head of a major corporation and entrusted with the authority to make million-dollar decisions, can never figure out what to wear on weekends, when he favors matching tan pants and shirts that make him look like, as she says, "the gasman—all he needs is an emblem on his pocket." She is a busy woman with a career of her own, too busy to lay out his clothes like a valet. "I can't stand it," she says. "With everything else I have to do, I shouldn't also have to buy his clothes and dress him."

Once, when they were newly married and he came downstairs ready to take a walk in their city neighborhood, she said she heard herself telling him, as if he were a child, "You can't go out like that."

"Why not?" he asked her seriously, perplexed. "I couldn't tell him he looked like a jerk," she says, laughing at the thirty-year-old memory. To his credit, he must have understood, because he went back inside and came out a few minutes later wearing the same outfit, this time with a cummerbund and formal dinner jacket. They both laughed. And stayed home. (I wish I had a twenty-dollar bill for every couple I know who has fought over clothes before they arrived at a party.)

Most of the women I know who dress their husbands say suits and shirts and ties aren't hard, since the uniform principle applies. It's the weekend wear that gets them down. That factor may be why a lot of men have adopted a sort of weekend uniform. There's the velour jumpsuit crowd, the shirt unbuttoned-down-to-here crowd, and the preppies who make it simple by wearing their too-old-to-wear-to-work-but-too-good-to-toss blue oxford-cloth shirts with chinos. Some men, the ones with cute bottoms and flat bellies, look darling in jeans and a nicely tailored shirt dressed up with a sweater or down vest in winter. It is wise to note here that young men, under thirty or so, are more confident about clothes. They dance better too, and these facts taken together say something about the evolution of the American male.

But for every husband who has an acceptable, standard weekend uniform, I have a friend married to a guy who likes to wear sweatpants with the peach-and-green print shirt his parents sent him last Christmas, which she keeps hiding in the back of his closet. He wears the shirt tucked in.

City Life

JANICE ROSENBERG

Any time of day, when I step onto my tiny front patio, I experience the sensuousness of city life. Garbage trucks wheeze and clang their backup warnings. The aroma of roasting coffee beans drifts toward me from a nearby shop. A driver shouts at a deliveryman to move his truck out of the frigging way. Mumbling to herself, a woman dressed in a housecoat and mules wanders slowly up the block. A man in spiffy slacks and blazer heads toward the bus stop. Skateboarders pass with their clop-clop horse-hoof sound. Cars with radios tuned to rap music are double-parked next door. A friend strolling back from the fruit-and-nut shop just up the street stops to say hello and offers me pistachio nuts. While tall trees shade me, I sip iced tea and lean back in my lawn chair, perfectly relaxed.

Back in the fifties, my parents believed that a home in the suburbs had every advantage over city life. Until I was nine, my family lived in Chicago in a five-room apartment. My mother and father, both of whom grew up in small towns, had no intention of staying in the city any longer than absolutely necessary. As soon as they had the means, they started looking for a house.

I remember the day my father told us, with obvious excitement, about the lot he had bought. He sketched his ideas for the house, then spent hours with an architect going over blueprints. On weekends we drove through suburbs checking out brick colors, stone trim, and landscaping styles. That winter I watched our house grow from a hole in the ground to a concrete-lined hole, and then watched as two-by-fours defined the rooms. I watched walls form out of heavy lathing and plaster and watched the stairs climb up and down. I tried out a level the bricklayers left behind, kept my hands away from freshly wired light switches, and saw plumbing pipe stacks becoming bathrooms, all the while wondering what life in the suburbs would be like.

The morning after we moved in I went outside to have a look around. I sat on the front step waiting for something to happen. I remembered city friends—riding scooters, kicking the can at an alley crossroad, climbing fences, playing winter king of the mountain and summer freeze tag. How could the mystique of alleys, with their labyrinthine world of garages and gangways, transfer to our suburb?

My brother and I had often sat on the step in front of our apartment building watching traffic on the busy street. We counted two-tone cars. Or he would count Buicks and I would count Fords in silly competition. Here, in our suburb, the few cars that appeared inevitably pulled into driveways. In the city, when my brother and I would grow tired of the front step, we would repair to our gray-painted third-floor back porch. There we would aim our peashooters at windows across the alley. We listened for garbage trucks and the vegetable peddler's horse-drawn anachronism. Here, our back yard faced other equally dull back yards. The garbage men arrived on Thursday mornings only. No kids stood below our windows hollering for my brother or me to come out and play.

So I waited. I missed the penny candy store, the corner grocery with German potato salad and Jewish rye bread where the owners knew me by name, and the landlord's tiny garden, from which I sampled fresh mint and basil. I thought about the drugstore with its soda fountain and its homemade black raspberry ice cream (in season only), and the empty lot with crab apple trees to climb.

On a late June day like this in the city, my mother would have taken me to the large wading pool in a nearby park. On weekend afternoons my father would have taken me to a different park, one near the Sinclair station. "Daddy's park" had a set of chinning bars. If my brother came along, my father pitched balls for us to hit.

On hot summer evenings in the city, my father treated us to Neapolitan ice cream, which the four of us shared. Since our refrigerator's only freezer was a box that held ice cube trays, we had to eat all the ice cream at once. My mother would slice the pint into four pieces. Then we'd sit around the kitchen table adding Hershey's syrup, nuts, banana slices, and maraschino cherries. Such evenings of togetherness seemed unlikely now that we had a giant freezer in our basement.

On Sundays in the city we had picnicked in a park with my aunts and uncles and cousins, or held autumn wienie roasts in forest preserves. Thinking of our new barbecue grill and the at-home parties it would certainly inspire, I understood that other changes were inevitable.

That first day at our new house, feeling nostalgic for the good old days, I waited on the front step for something to happen. The mailman walked by and said hello. Inside, my mother papered cabinets. For her, moving from a third-floor apartment to a house offered the ultimate advantage: She would not have to run down three flights of stairs to tighten my roller skates or drag my bicycle out of the basement. She would not have to keep me busy upstairs with paper dolls and empty grocery cartons while she did the housework. Clearly, her days as my entertainment committee had ended.

When we'd been in our new house for about a week, a girl my age rang the back doorbell. Her mother had seen me sitting on our patio wall. Did I want to go to her house and play? Desperate for company, I went.

She became the first of many neighborhood pals. Trusting the safety of our suburb, our parents let us roam. They had moved out of the city so that we could play on lawns instead of in alleys rife with broken glass and dog dirt. They had checked the suburb carefully for playgrounds and had converted basement into recreation rooms complete with Ping-Pong tables and shuffleboard grids.

But we ignored their pale offerings of suburban recreation. As if to satisfy some primitive need, we sought adventure, courted danger. First-generation suburbanites, we had yet to learn the pleasures of hanging out at indoor shopping malls. Instead we explored the empty lots around our houses, climbed trees, and ate unidentified berries. We built illicit clubhouses with bent nails and wood stolen from construction sites. We trotted down the railroad tracks in search of unnamed treasure. We trespassed on half-finished houses, climbing the wobbly planks that served as temporary stairways.

Suburban streets were meant to protect us from excess traffic, but our bike rides naturally brought us to the most heavily traveled thoroughfares. Ignoring our parents' imperatives that we cross at the light, we dashed through fast-moving traffic to the drugstore on the nearest commercial street in search of grape bubble gum and trading cards. Rather than walk three blocks to the park, we organized softball games in intersections. When police patrol cars rolled into view, we ran like robbers from the scene; then, thrilled with our own daring, we returned minutes later to resume our game.

Back in the fifties we played happily in our new suburb, became teenagers, explored the city, and decided where we wanted to live with families of our own. When I came home from college in New York City, I discovered that the peaceful quiet of suburban streets and the repetitive split-level houses bored me. When I looked out my window, I wanted to see not static landscapes but things happening. When I walked around my neighborhood I wanted to see people on the street. I craved the sensuous variety of city life. So I moved back to Chicago and stayed.

Years ago my father gave up suggesting that my husband and I buy a house in the suburbs for our family. As for my friends who claim they've moved to the suburbs "for the kids," well, let me just say that clean sidewalks don't count for much if no one ever takes a walk. Knowing that kids find adventure and danger wherever they live, I chose city life for myself.

This choice, which I once thought selfish, has not hurt my children. In fact, I think it has been good for them. When they were small, we strolled to lakeshore playgrounds filled with kids and parents. While growing up, they discovered the sneaky pleasure of shortcut climbs over back fences. They played ball with a gang of neighborhood kids—a mixed lot if I ever saw one—that claimed a particular driveway as their territory no matter how many times they were chased away by janitors and landlords. Lacking the automatic protection of yellow school buses, they learned to avoid drunks and loud jabberers on city buses by sitting up front. When my younger son's cousins expressed frightened concern over the number of blacks, he shook his head sadly at their obvious prejudice. When a suburban friend gaped at the homosexuals and lesbians in our neighborhood, my older son scoffed at his lack of sophistication. Since the day my sons saw a man with gold hoop earrings dangling from his pierced nipples, neither of them notices any but the most outlandish transvestite.

My mother sometimes bemoaned the lack of casual interaction among the neighbors on her suburban street. No one took walks. They went directly from house to garage to car. Bushes shielded back yard patios from one another. Front porches were what she missed most from her Southern small-town childhood.

I remember summer visits to my grandparents' house in

Tennessee, spending hot nights in the glider on their screened-in porch, engulfed by the scent of honeysuckle and the rhythmic song of crickets. My street has more in common with that town than any modern suburb ever can. When I think of ubiquitous central air conditioning and closed-up suburban houses as I spend an evening sipping iced tea on my front step, I am glad I have come home to the city.

VISIONS OF
MASTERY

$\mathcal{K}$nives

CARROLL STONER

Learning to use a knife is the single most important step you can take toward having authority in the kitchen. It is the very symbol of self-assurance. Once you know how to use cutlery, you will become fearless. Using a good knife in the kitchen is the closest most of us will ever come to swashbuckling. Watch your knife separate the chicken leg from its connecting thigh with one definitive movement. Feel it angle the bottoms of tough peony stems with a resounding thud on the butcher block. Watch it fly through crisp vegetables for a stir-fried dish that rivals a Chinese restaurant's in its speed of delivery.

Yet, like a surgeon, the woman behind a sharp knife can be gentle. See it slide through a ripe tomato without exerting so much as a small squeeze, and losing only a minimum of precious juice.

Wielding a good knife, of course, is flirting with danger. When newly sharpened knives slide effortlessly through a chicken joint, they will cut just as easily through a fingertip or newly manicured nail. Knives are not for the weak of heart. In the first days of cutlery use, you will see blood, and some of it may be your own.

Keep at it, though, because once you can use a knife with the skill of a professional chef you will have a feeling of accomplishment like no other—a feeling both physically and intellectually satisfying. If you want to judge a cook's genuine expertise and degree of confidence in the kitchen, watch her sharpen her knives.

I have no compunction about wielding my knives, either in the kitchen or in public, perhaps because my father taught me everything I know. He must have believed that carving is not related to gender or he would not have taught me at all. Now, with the confidence he helped nurture, I can see that women shouldn't use their knives with dexterity in privacy only to relinquish them at the moment of public triumph. If you can stuff and roast a goose, you can carve it.

Every time he came to visit, my father made a beeline for the kitchen and inevitably made me laugh, albeit a little impatiently. He would say, with mock disapproval, "You could ride to China on these knives." What he was saying was that my knives were dull, too dull to be useful. Then he would ceremoniously take out the long, thin butcher's steel he had bought me, anchor the point on his hip, and proceed to sharpen my knives one by one. This was about as close as I ever saw him come to swaggering. He sharpened those knives like a pirate.

What kind of knives do you need? Just as the best clothing is made of real fibers such as silk, linen, wool, and cotton, the finest knives have no plastic or falsely shiny metal on them. They have tempered carbon-steel blades that are firmly attached to solid, hefty wooden handles or to plastic-impregnated wood. The metal from the blade extends through the handle, either partway or all the way. This feature is called the "tang," and knives are said to have "full tang" when metal extends all the way to the end of the handle. For all but the biggest knives, "partial tang" will mean a good, serviceable knife. The biggest ones, including the chef's knife, need "full tang" for weight, balance, and durability.

Before buying a knife, hold it in your hand. Feel the weight and assess the knife's balance. How does it fit in your palm? If it doesn't feel right (and this is difficult to assess, since a beginning cook won't know what feeling "right" is), try another with a blade and handle that give you a feeling of solidity and comfort. This feeling is what you are looking for when you buy. Ultimately, in your collection of knives, one or two will become favorites because of the way they work and the way they feel.

As for quantity, think of your knives the way a Parisian regards her wardrobe. Start with the best basics you can afford. Learn to use them well. Then and only then should you add to your collection. Begin with a large carving knife, a paring knife, and one with a long, thin blade. Like your good black dress, each of these should be of the best quality you can afford. Add to this beginner's set a long, serrated knife for cutting bread, cake, and certain fine-grained meats such as ham.

Along the way, you'll also want some inexpensive variety knives such as the curved and serrated time-saving grape-fruit knife, the shrimp deveiner, the potato peeler, and several other knifelike tools. As for electric knives, they are in the same category as the hotdogger and electric wok—unnecessary because the simplest way of doing things in the kitchen is usually the best.

Learn to use your knives. First, practice basic skills such as slicing evenly and chopping rapidly. When slicing celery for Chinese food, for example, all the pieces should be the same size. When slicing a beef tongue, the most difficult meat to cut evenly, learn to angle the cuts, so it looks hand-cut rather than machine-cut but still moderately neat.

As you slice, experiment with your knife. Bang it dramatically onto the surface as you cut through many stalks of celery at once. Aim the point down and cut only with the widest part of your knife. Strive for a rhythm that feels right. Don't be overcautious. Be aware that working with a sharp knife is less dangerous than with a dull one, since you won't need to exert as much pressure. Work slowly at first, but when you have found a style of cutting that works, speed it up.

Chopping works best when done rapidly, and then it's both

flashy and fun. Chopping an onion with a chef's technique is a display of competence. Quickly move the knife up and down, holding the tip firmly on the board. Faster now, and then faster again. Practice until you impress yourself with your prowess. The fast-chopping movement with a large, well-sharpened carving knife never fails to satisfy.

The money you put into good knives will be repaid many times over. Knowing how to use your knife means you can bone a chicken breast in the time it takes to decide whether you should pay three times the normal price to have your butcher do it for you. It means inviting friends over at the last minute for an elegant or dashing meal. With your butcher knife, you can carve a whole stuffed veal breast or crown roast in front of awed guests.

But the most important reason to learn to use your knives is also the simplest: the knife is the cook's single most important tool. Without it you can't understand the structure, the texture, the very character of food: the fiber of celery, the spring of a fresh mushroom, the impenetrability of squash, the succulence of a perfectly ripe tomato. Without knowing the essence of food, you cannot be creative in its preparation.

The cook who can't use a knife is no cook at all.

Power

LAURA GREEN

By the time most people have been married for a decade, the fights about sex should be winding down. Either there was nothing to fight about in the first place, or you outgrew the problem, or you got a divorce for a whole bunch of reasons, or you threw in the towel and put your energy somewhere else.

All too often, especially in the early seventies when the women's movement led a lot of us to demand what Aretha Franklin called our propers, the bed was a hellacious battleground. But then, again, the bed has always been a Russian front for the obstinate. Sex provides plenty of tinder—and as long as most couples are fighting, they figure what the hell, they might as well be efficient and fight about everything that's bothering them. At least, that's the way we always did it. Our fights degenerated into impressive power struggles. But aren't all fights in a marriage over power?

Assuming the center of the marriage holds, time will save the bed. Time turns it back into a place you can crawl into, muss up the pillows, and read peacefully in. But not for me, not always. I'm married to a man who is back in grad school and working full time, so there are days we almost never see each other. We have to talk business in bed, and that inevitably leads us to the kind of infuriated quarreling that comes from two people, three jobs, and three kids.

"Did you pay your tuition this month?"

93

His magazine rustles slightly, like a trapped deer quivering in the bushes. I know he is pretending he didn't hear me and he probably knows I know this. I should take the hint. I should write the damned check myself. I know this.

"Did you?"

"Uh, probably not."

"Why not?"

"I had a busy day."

"Dammit, we'll get behind again."

No answer.

"Jesus Christ," I snap. "I'll pay it. But this was supposed to be your job."

This is what it has come down to. After all the fights over who controls this and who controls that, neither of us wants to do any of it. Not the bookkeeping. Not the check reconciling. Not the calling the bank. What we want to do is make the grand decisions and let someone else look after the details.

Power is not the power to do, I have learned, but the power to make someone else do it.

The checkbook is as good an example as any. I have struggled with math my whole life and have never been able to balance a checkbook properly. Over the years the fudge factor I can live with has grown. Early on I decided I could tolerate $35 discrepancies, then $50 errors, then, finally, mistakes of as much as $300. But it was an uneasy tolerance and I felt guilty that I couldn't do a better job. I know I shouldn't have felt guilty, but I did. I kept trying to make the numbers work out, but I was always off.

Then my husband and I got married and decided to have one checking account, making the kind of mistake only newlyweds would make. I may not have done the math right, but he didn't even enter the checks. He took money out with his bankcard and didn't record it. He grabbed checks at random from unused check pads and never told me. He was like some impoverished aristocrat in his disdain for the mundane, petty details of money-grubbing life, and I became the bureau-

crat nipping at his patrician heels. His money blindness alternately drove me to ham-handed sarcasm ("See this little square?
Enter the amount in pencil—you *do* know what a pencil is,
right?") or to blind fury ("Get the fuck out of my life!"). It was
an open-and-shut case of no respect. If he had valued bookkeeping and respected the process of it, he would have entered
the damned checks. I didn't understand it then, but he was
exercising the power to delegate. He got to mess; I got to clean
up. And that's what infuriated me.

A partial answer, embarrassing in its simplicity, was separate checking accounts. That way he had to live with his own
messes. I would have done it sooner except that I was operating on the principle that husbands and wives should share
everything in their lives. As a practical matter, he kept the
checking account with the status—the one whose check numbers had rolled over into five digits. It was such a mare's nest
by then that the only thing it was still good for was walk-
around money. I opened a new account with checks numbered
in the measly three-digits, just like a twenty-one-year-old on
her first job. But at least I had a clean slate.

I kept the house accounts and my personal spending in one
joint account; he wrote occasional checks out of his account.
From time to time he'd pull one of my checks from the box in
my desk and forget what he wrote it for. I would holler when
it came in and he would apologize contritely. I balanced my
checkbook and paid the bills. He stuffed them in envelopes
and put the stamps on.

Investing the money was my job, too. At first I cleared
decisions with him. Then I would tell him what I had done.
Old habits die hard, including the habit of thinking women
shouldn't handle the big stuff. I finally stopped filling him in
about matters he didn't want to know about last year. We had
an uneven distribution of labor and an inequitable system, but
it wobbled along. I had power, I thought, and I was willing to
put in the time to keep it.

The truth was a lot more convoluted. Any power I had was

power by default, power without respect—and that is not power but responsibility. He had no interest in the job, considered it scut work, and left me to do it. The same process of devaluing work when women do it operates in the job market. Once women start entering a profession in any numbers, the salaries freeze and sometimes decline. Look at public relations.

Like the medieval pilgrim, I took two steps forward and one step back. Managing the family money had degenerated into bird-dogging the paperwork. It was another household chore, like folding laundry. While I struggled through the fat file folder labeled "Unpaid Bills," my husband stretched out on the couch watching movies with names like *Death Helicopter*. He took it easy; I was alligator wrestling with the Mastercard.

Listening to the murmur of the television, I have to admit that I confused authority (the power to make people do things) with responsibility (the obligation to do them). Since I'm stuck with the job, I've done two things to make my life easier. I told my husband that since I handle the money, he has to handle the grocery shopping. "Sure," he said. "Just make me a list." Having learned my lesson about delegating work, I told him uh-uh, that was his job now, and I showed him where the grocery list pad was. Then I decided to operate on a need-to-know basis, the grown-up equivalent of playing chicken. The need-to-know approach is simple. If you don't absolutely have to know it, then don't.

Ever since this summer, my husband and I joke a lot about the need to know. We learned about the way it could simplify life the day my daughter left for camp with a friend. Her father was supposed to drive them up; we would bring them back. He showed up at the right time, loaded the trunks into the car, and then asked, "Now where am I going?"

We dug out the maps of Michigan. We traced his route to the town nearest the camp—a seven-hour drive across three states. He said he'd ask for directions to the camp when he got closer. I must have looked astonished because he said, "I always operate on a need-to-know basis." He fished in his pocket for the slip of paper his wife had given him with the name of the motel where they were to spend the night, waved goodbye, and drove off. My kids said they went around in circles some, but he got them where they had to go.

I haven't completely abandoned my bean counting, just the hard part—just the stuff I don't absolutely need to know, like how much money is actually in there. As long as there's enough, I'm satisfied. To that end, I enter the checks in the checkbook and tot up the amounts from time to time. When I think I am running out of money, I call the bank for a quick chat with accounting. Between now and next April 15, I may do something about the canceled checks. Or I may not. I save a lot of time.

I am not alone. A banker I know tells me that 90 percent of the professionals who bank with her, including a few CPAs, don't balance their checkbooks. "They let a month go by, and that's it," she says. It's the opposite of smoking. Once they quit, it's hard to start again.

I know a man who has never balanced his checkbook. I know a man who rounds off every check to the next highest dollar so he'll be sure to put in extra money. I know several people who put money in their accounts but don't write it down so they have a cushion against error. I know a man who opens new checking accounts every eighteen months because that's how long it takes for his record keeping to get completely out of control. I know a man with a $1,000 line of credit to cover the glitches. The banker says this messy accounting happens all the time and that men are worse than women when it comes to checkbooks. "Women try harder to keep it straight. Men have less patience and won't spend the time."

I wonder if men didn't wink at each other as their newly liberated wives offered to take over the family finances. It must have been a great opportunity—keep an option to control the big decisions and delegate the responsibility for the scut work. Sometimes as I watched my husband, with his eyes on the television and his feet on the table, I wondered if the guys hadn't played a Tom Sawyer on us. Did they wink and say, "Ooh, I don't know, it's awfully hard work?" when we looked over their shoulders and offered to help? Old Tom knew that people only wanted to paint the fence if it was an important job. But since it's not, I'm learning to appreciate a good whitewash.

Thrift

NANCY EBERLE

A woman who shall be nameless decided one winter day to clean the cupboards beneath her bathroom sink. The cupboard on the left side she used for towels, which she took pleasure in keeping paired by color with the folded edge facing front. The cupboard to the right was the ship's hold, the belly of the beast, the bathroom's basement—a jumble of sprays for hair and sprays for boots, sprays for bugs and sprays for bites, witch hazel for forgotten injuries and shoe polish for forgotten shoes. When she reached the innermost wall, she found a small, neatly folded paper bag nestled beneath the U-shaped drain. Inside was a pregnancy testing kit, its cellophane seal unbroken. Although she was fifty-two and three years past her last period, her hand hovered over the wastebasket. How could she throw away something unopened, something worth, according to the drugstore price tag, $10.99? Her hand hovered, and having hovered moved on. She stuffed it back under the drainpipe.

Thrift may be responsible for more cluttering up of our home lives than any other attitude.
Thrift is:

- deciding the placemats are clean enough to use one more time, and discovering they aren't when you take them out to set the table for company.

- leaving the dirty dishes in the dishwasher in the morning because there weren't enough to do a load, and finding in the evening that there aren't enough to set the table, either.

- buying only one pair of tights for your daughter when you finally find her size although you know they're going to run on first wearing—and of course, they do.

Because of thrift we save clothes too good to throw away (but too unattractive to wear); books for which we have no affection (and no shelf space); double bed sheets (although our bed is now queen-size); dibs and dabs of leftover food (although we haven't used up last week's), and a hundred other items that clog our drawers, closets, desks, and above all, our minds. Because of thrift we go without basics (like a decent paring knife), buy one of something when we need two (like a lipstick for home and purse), and buy two when we need a dozen (like pens and postage stamps).

What makes us so crimped, so cramped, so constipated? How do our houses get to be junkyards and our selves wandering Ophelias within them, when all we ever wanted was simplicity and order? Why is it so difficult to buy what we need with a clear conscience?

The truth of the matter is that thrift is not so closely linked to income as is commonly assumed, and is perhaps more closely linked to gender than imagined. Like the beauty who always sees herself as the fat little girl she was in third grade, women carry with them their economic pasts. We carry thrift in our collective unconscious as the historic keepers of the hearth, and we carry it in individual memories as the result of our personal histories.

We are the kindergartner with a nickel clutched in her fist and a quarter's worth of candy dreams; we are the teenager with never enough clothes or makeup; we are the newly married and proud of our prudence; we are the single parent trying to make it without any child support. With layer upon layer of values, is it any wonder that when we are about to buy something, the voices come rushing forth, a dissonant chorus? "Buy it?" "Don't be ridiculous—I can't afford it!" "You deserve it." "But I'll feel so guilty. . . ." Nor does this internal warfare always end at the edge of the combat zone. Often it follows us home, tarnishing whatever pleasure we may have taken in our purchase.

The same process takes place when we go to throw something away. One self decisively dumps the contents of the junk drawer on the kitchen table, with the intention of returning it to its place in pristine condition. Other selves, like a clutch of greedy children, beg to keep three-quarters of its contents. At bottom we all carry within us respect for the intrinsic value of things. It's the same sensibility that makes our children gasp when we throw away a piece of jewelry with a broken clasp or a pair of spike heels from the back of the closet. They have no jewelry, no heels, few possessions of any kind. Things are wonderful, in and of themselves.

And then there are the admonitions of the past: waste not, want not; clean your plate; think of all the starving children in India; your father works hard to put this food on the table; when I was a child I would have been glad . . . We are like our houses, full of old goods that we are unable to throw away.

The result of all this clamor is not, unfortunately, a simple and steady standard against which to test our longing to get and to keep but a generalized feeling of "shouldn't"—shouldn't buy, shouldn't throw away—that makes us feel guilty and clogs our houses with what we don't need even as it prevents us from buying what we do.

So what do we do about it? How to allot these voices their say, bearing in mind that among them is the voice of conscience, without going through life paralyzed by indecision? We have to come to terms with the concept of thrift itself. Thrift is not a virtue. Thrift is a set of economies wrongly elevated to a philosophy that tips life out of balance in the direction of deprivation and accumulation simultaneously—no mean trick.

Unexamined thrift in a society where planned obsolescence is the rule is a formula for suffocating in your own detritus. Saving old clothes is not a virtue; getting them to a shelter for the homeless is. Keeping old furniture in the attic is not a virtue. Selling it at a garage sale so it can be recycled to another family is. Saving styrofoam meat trays is not a virtue. Buying less meat—which is an inefficient use of the world's grain supply—is.

We must rethink the meaning of thrift, upgrading it from the small frugalities required by a pioneer society to the larger husbandry demanded by the diminishing resources of our planet. What does this have to do with our closets? Everything. It challenges the knee-jerk response "Never throw anything away." It frees us to think about what we're doing. Buying in multiples often makes sense—so does not buying at all. And finally, by liberating us from all that guilt, true thrift frees our energy for more important issues. If we can clean out our closets, maybe we can clean up the universe.

Conflict

LAURIE ABRAHAM

When I was nine, I informed my mother that I would never live in a home like hers. I didn't know how to arrange dried flowers, or buy drapes that matched the couch, or prepare meals that matched the dishes. I didn't know how, and I refused to learn. My mother smiled knowingly and said, "You're a smart girl. I'll be very surprised if you don't want to end up in a place where you can appreciate your surroundings." More smiles. "But it's your choice."

From that point on, I rarely lost an opportunity to tell my mother, or anyone who cared to listen, how much I detested things domestic. I also played house a good deal. I carefully arranged my favorite dishes in an olive-green hutch built by Uncle Lester, adorned the walls of our basement playroom with *National Geographic* photos, and propped fat-cheeked dolls in high-chairs for meals of plastic steak and potatoes. By junior high, I had given up this game, but I had definite ideas about how the only part of the house I controlled—my bedroom—would be decorated. My sister opted for a mix of bright oranges and yellows. I chose wallpaper with lavender and apple-green flowers, a deep purple shag carpet, and a matching chenille bedspread. My room became a display case for a substantial collection of knickknacks. No surface was spared, but most of my possessions were arranged on a glass-shelved vanity that had been in my mother's bedroom when she was a girl. When I cleaned, I cleared off one shelf at a time, dusting each object individually— the blown-glass cat from the Ohio State Fair, the cherubic china girl from my grandmother, and the candle in the shape of an ice cream sundae purchased with allowance money from Wicks and Sticks. It never occurred to me as I grew up that while I pronounced homemaking trivial, I was an ardent homemaker. Only lately have I had to face up to my desire to create a real home, for I am living with someone who is obsessed with it.

Paul has owned only one copy of *Playboy* in the six years I have known him, but he has stacks of old issues of *Casa Vogue*, *Interior Design*, *Architectural Digest*, *Arbitaire*, and *La Maison*. (He does *not* own *Better Homes and Gardens*, a magazine I have learned to regard as the Sears store of the design magazine world.) Occasionally, he'll buy an especially "succulent" new issue of one of these magazines, but most of them are beyond his budget. Instead, he spends a few hours each week flipping through current issues in drugstores, checking out unique moldings while his more carnal brothers drool over centerfolds. Paul's fascination with creating our home seemed at first to fit my needs neatly. It was a match made in a modern woman's heaven: Paul decorates the house and I work twelve hours a day.

That arrangement has not worked. My female friends look at me in horror when I tell them that Paul won't let me hang a certain picture. My friends make the art and furniture choices in their homes. Liz, for instance, picked out the white couch in the living room and the Georgia O'Keeffe prints on the wall by herself, and she won't allow her boyfriend to hang an original drawing of a transvestite that he bought in New Orleans. She will be the arbiter of taste in her home. I can't be. Paul is encroaching on the one area where women traditionally have prevailed, and I'm embarrassed by my lack of design acumen. The modern woman does it all, job *and* home, but I can't even pick out a $1.49 dish towel without worrying about Paul's reaction.

On some level, I know I should just forget about traditional sex roles and consider myself lucky that someone else is doing the decorating. I want to let go, but I can't. I'm beginning to admit to myself the truth of my mother's wisdom: People need to appreciate their surroundings. There is another problem, however. People don't always appreciate the same surroundings, and some appreciate surroundings more passionately than others.

I've tried to downplay the different appreciations, or tastes, that Paul and I have. I didn't really think I *had* taste, anyway; I just knew which objects I liked. How could Paul object to the small, framed picture of my mother I wanted to put on my desk, or the glass sculpture she gave me for my birthday? These objects were important to me. But Paul is a design dogmatist. He sees the house as a whole, and one inappropriate piece of pottery can upset the balance. He also rejects the home in which he grew up, and my nostalgic possessions remind him of it.

Most of our decorating arguments are the same: I want to alter our environment with an object; Paul wants it to be as empty as possible, save for a few pieces he considers unusual. He hates anything that is remotely trendy or middle-class, anything that "the Joneses" might own. His divorced mother never could keep up with that standard-setting family. Instead, right after moving into a new ranch house, she told her four children that she could not afford to maintain it. "Our house started out a bright yellow," Paul has told me several times. "Then the paint peeled off until it was a chalky white, and an old coat of pink started showing through. I couldn't see out of my bedroom window because the bushes were too high." His friends teased him, and he remembers feeling ashamed, wishing for a freshly painted home and a neat yard. On weekend visits to his father's custom-decorated apartment, he acquired his love for decorating magazines. When his sisters and father were watching TV, he'd slip off and dream with the latest issue of *Architectural Digest*.

I come to the task of decorating with my own set of memories and expectations. I grew up believing that my mother's taste in wallpaper, in knickknacks, even in dried flowers, was flawless. In my own place, I feel guilty when I no longer appreciate the dried-flower arrangements she loves; I was taught to know the difference between ugly ones and pretty ones. The bad arrangements were sold at high-priced, low-quality gift shops; the good ones she made and were set about our house, changing with the seasons. I appreciated them then, so why not now? My devotion to dried flowers is similar to how I felt about my younger sister when I was a little girl: I could belittle her or give her a kick, but neighborhood kids had better not dare to do the same. Paul has said that certain objects, including certain dried-flower arrangements, "insult" him. "Well," I retort, "your being insulted by dried flowers insults me and my mother."

Exposing the origins of the separate designs Paul and I have on our home has been a useful exercise, to an extent. Not that knowing why we like what we like and hate what we hate has fused our decorating visions. I always will have trouble standing up to a man whom I believe to be an inspired artist, a man who has studied the last twenty years of *Architectural Digest*. But discovering each other's early influences has given us ground, shifting though it be, for compromise. Last night I suggested we buy a small rug to lie in front of the sink, where the floor is splintered and pocked and perpetually spotted by water. I imagined a rug in neutral tones, something that wouldn't show the dirt. Paul smiled condescendingly.

"I don't want to break up the floor. I like the even color."

What harm could come from a tiny, neutral throw rug placed discreetly in front of the sink? "My mother bought them at Zayre's. Every couple of months, there would be a new one in front of the sink, some cheery yellow," Paul spits.

Or perhaps that's our ground for compromise. If we buy a rug, it will be gray. Two shades of gray if I'm lucky.

Family Stories

LAURA GREEN

The little I know about my mother's father I learned at the kitchen sink while doing the dishes with my mother. Since that was the only time she talked about him, her infrequent recollections produced my funny, hybrid memories. When I think of him, I think of doing the glasses before the silverware as often as I think of the time he tore his pants climbing through the front-room window. My recollections are embellished by the steamy warmth of the water in the cold kitchen, the chilly linoleum floor, and the black night outside the kitchen window. I never knew my grandfather's voice, so instead of a thick Eastern European accent with broad *A*'s and missing *th*'s, his sound is the clink of silverware.

My grandfather died about ten years before I was born. The official cause of death was kidney failure, but my mother said the Depression killed him. A real estate man of sorts, he lost it all in the crash. My mother used to say that if he had only lived a few years longer, he would have made it back. Then the house would have been the way she always described it, filled with people laughing and arguing around the dining room table, books in three or four languages on the shelves, gypsy music or Tchaikovsky or something just as overtly romantic and sentimental coming from the record player. But he died and my mother was on her own and broke. She plunged into the politics of the thirties and became the woman she was meant to be.

The nights we did the dishes, I had my mother all to myself—a rarity, since she was often doing office business on the phone or curled up in her chair writing something on a legal pad when she wasn't at her office. Doing the dishes was a time of truce in our often acrimonious relationship. I didn't whine about boys and she didn't get on my case about paying too much attention to what she considered the trivialities of popularity. Instead, she talked to me like a grown-up about grown-up things. Some of it was office stuff about coping with an independent collection of colleagues. She also told family stories, with the best parts heavily edited, about the peccadillos of her admirable, oddball clan.

Running through her stories like a dealer slapping down the cards, she laid out her philosophy—a full-steam-ahead, don't-look-back, give-'em-hell, sez-who? approach that was fascinating to absorb, though daunting to imitate. Looking at the pack through her eyes (and there was no other way to view them) was a lesson in how a woman ought to manage her life. Mostly, she said, it should be without interference, because you know best. What she didn't say, because she didn't have to say it, was that I would know best because I was her daughter and no daughter of hers would be wimpy or wishy-washy.

My mother died more than a decade ago, about the time I got the worst of the wimpiness out of my system. My daughter is the same age as I was when my mother told me family stories. Sometimes we sprawl out on the couch and she puts her head on my shoulder. She's supposed to be doing homework and I ought to be grading papers, but I talk about my mother and grandmother.

I tell my own variations of the family stories for the same reasons my mother did: to be companionable, to give her pride in her family, and to teach her to love the things I love. They are subtle lessons and need reinforcement through repetition.

You cannot tell a child, "Love reading. Be bold." Children learn attitudes by understanding what is important to their parents and then, we hope, by emulating it out of a desire to please. Once my mother and I were at the ballet. I was sitting on the edge of my seat, waiting for the dancers to begin. She whispered, "Your grandfather used to lean forward like that. He loved ballet. You're just like him." Her voice was full of affection and approval.

My daughter's favorite story is about the time my mother sent the governor of Michigan a snake. I don't remember the details—what the governor had done that ran counter to the interests of the union she headed—though I do remember a brief, vivid uproar. The missing details don't bother my daughter. She loves her grandmother's boldness. In telling her the story the way I do, approvingly, I am giving her permission to be bold.

There is nothing like family stories for passing on family values. What we choose to remember (and what we bury like the dead) says a great deal about who we are and what we want to be. Family stories were my mother's metaphors, her way of putting ideas into a context a thirteen-year-old could understand. She stood on her side of the sink, a short, stout woman in a pair of plain slacks and a ratty, tan sweater, arms deep in hot water. Other mothers may have talked about boys and clothes; mine analyzed the marriages in the family. She told me who was social climbing and who cheated. She knew which were love matches and which weren't. She glossed over the juicy parts and passed on truths—her truths, anyway—about men, women, and values. If it sounds as though she lectured, she didn't. But she was quick to judge and she made her views clear.

My mother's family was a quirky, intelligent lot, good at what they did, charming, and sometimes exceedingly hard to get along with. They taught me how to play chess poorly, adore Edith Piaf, cry at sentimental movies, love books, and appreciate debate so competitive that my oldest friend used to say that Sunday brunch at my house was great training for real life.

My grandfather was a charmer, I was told, with sharp, sparkly black eyes and a beefy walrus mustache. In the one picture I remember of him, he looks fat, prosperous, and curious, a man who would have been at home in Freud's Vienna or Renoir's Paris. The stories my mother told about him were not of adventure, but of repartee, about what you'd expect of a turn-of-the-century businessman. One of her favorites was about the summer when she and her friends, her brother and sister and their friends, and her parents and their friends argued for weeks about which was the true revolution, the Russian or the French. I can see them and hear them, sitting on the edges of their broad, wooden lawn chairs, oblivious to the mosquitoes, tense as relay runners waiting for the perfect second to jump in and grab the batons. Everybody is talking at once, or trying to. The debate advances and circles back upon itself, a stubborn dialogue in English and Yiddish. She loved that story the way she loved a good argument. My forebears were talkers, not artists, but they also respected art.

My mother also told what I have come to think of as the great Stanislavsky story. (I should say right off that I don't believe it's true because it's too good to be true.)

According to my mother, her parents' house was a home away from home for Russian and Yiddish artists traveling through the Midwest. She swore that my grandfather walked in the door one night with Konstantin Stanislavsky. When dinner was done, my grandmother insisted that the men do the dishes. My mother says there is a photo somewhere of the two men at the sink, sleeves rolled up, talking to pass the time. As I said, it's too good to be true, but it tells a lot about what mattered to her: the arts with a capital *A*, being unconventional, and having no qualms about making even the man who developed Method acting scrub the pots. She reenacted her ideas on my grandfather's stage.

The purpose of family stories is to give you ideas. Ideas of

who you are and will be, and of what will become of you.
Whether family stories are factual or not is beside the point.
Family stories are funny things. They're not about uncles and
dogs and picnics at all. They're part glue, binding generations
together, part behavior lessons, and part attempts to set the
past right.

The stories my mother told me about herself were moxie,
take-charge stories about the way she stepped in and ran
things after her father died. I came to admire her toughness, to
see it as a way of getting something done even if you had to
beat the thing senseless first. She told a lot of smart-kid
stories, making me glad I was a smart kid. She also told
bigmouth stories. I tried to be a bigmouth, and was slapped
down before I knew what hit me.

In this mobile century, when grandma is in Tucson and
Aunt May is thinking about the Peace Corps, family stories
are all we have of a personal past. In another time, our pasts
were all around us in our aunts and uncles and grandparents.
You couldn't *not* know who you were and what you were
expected to become. That was why so many young men and
women took off—to get away from their family histories and
reinvent themselves. But they still tucked away the old stories
in their memories, like pictures in the back of a drawer. And
when they pull out those stories years later, they are startled
by the resemblances to their own lives.

My mother has been dead fourteen years, my father and
grandmother twice that. My aunt died more than thirty years
ago and my grandfather nearly sixty. But I see them all, the
ones I knew and the ones I didn't know. I tell their stories to
my children so they can know at least something of them.
They belong in my house and my life. It is their house, too,
shaped in part by the influence of those stories. They would
like the clutter and the magazines, and my son's trombone and
the pot of coffee on the counter. They would approve of my
husband and fuss over the children. They would see that I
keep their mementos—my grandmother's carved Russian boxes,

a book from my aunt with her treasured note on the flyleaf, my father's tiny opera glasses.

They would feel comfortable in my house. They should; they helped make it the way it is.

The Pink Wall

CARROLL STONER

There is a wall in my living room that gives me pleasure every time I look at it. It is composed of a Chinese screen, a chaise longue, six black-and-white photographs, and a few fat Mexican pots. And it is pink.

It took me almost fifty years to design that wall.

First of all, the wall color is exactly what I wanted. I know. I know that pink is considered an insipid color, wimpy or simpy or overly sentimental. What I like about my wall is that it thumbs its nose at the notion of pink and goes it one better.

Pink was always my favorite color. When I was given the chance to choose colors for my first "decorated" bedroom when I was ten, I chose—you guessed it—pink. The candy-pink carpet was the height of daring back then, and neighbors raved about my mother's courage in putting a pastel rug in a child's room. But my mother was making a statement. As she used to say, "I trust my girls."

Over the years, I've been through a number of stages. First there was the all-white stage, with every wall a blank canvas to spotlight everything else in the room. Even those rooms with no architectural features whatsoever assume some dignity when painted white. I found it boring. Then there were pale-gray walls, and once, for a few years, a high-ceilinged living room painted bright, hot yellow with lots of plants and an Oriental rug. Another time there was a navy blue bedroom (and the same Oriental) that was as close to a womb as any room I've been in. They were nice experiments. But I wanted to cocoon myself in pink. For me, pink is the color of luxe, as in Palm Beach, Mexican sunsets, and the delight of pastel houses in the tropics. And there's that old, comforting childhood feeling.

The decision to live in a gray, northern American city surrounded by pink has to be intentional. I tried it first with pale-gray Berber-style rugs on hardwood floors, and I had a paint mixed that I thought would be perfect. It was disgusting. Lesson number one for pink lovers: All pinks look about fifteen times brighter on the wall than on the paint chip. I painted over my Pepto-Bismol pink wall the next night—it was too much of a failure to contemplate for longer than that.

Four years later, we moved to an apartment with a breathtaking view of water and sunrises on the uncluttered eastern horizon. One morning while I was visiting my empty, new apartment, Lake Michigan was the most beautiful shade of blue-green, a cool color that gave me a little jolt of pleasure every time I looked at it. I wanted that exact shade of blue in my home and decided to use it in rugs: A quiet, muted blue-green. But what color could I use on the walls with this subtle color? It had to be pink, the palest pink of the perfect sunrise.

This would take courage, maybe more than I possessed.

I'll cut to the chase and tell you that I pulled it off. We live in a pink house. I love it. Most friends say they like it, too. Some say nothing—and I don't ask. The secret to the color's success, and there is one, is that it isn't exactly pink, but a beige that on the paint chip bears no resemblance to anything rosy.

So part of my self-satisfaction (and I confess that's what it is) lies in the fact that I finally got the color right, that I could live in pink surroundings that weren't hopelessly revealing of what I feared was my true character—insipid, girly-girly, sweet as cotton candy. (Even my worst enemies wouldn't choose those terms to describe me.)

The other part of my sense of mastery is what hangs on and is in front of that perfect pink wall. On the left is a large Chinese folding screen that I had the guts to buy at an auction one Sunday afternoon, though I didn't know where I'd use it when I bought it. It was too costly to be a whim; I thought it would look wonderful with my black Mexican pots in front of it, and so I brought it home to try in different spots throughout the room. It worked. With a border of dull black lacquer (I can't prove it, but I think anything shiny and black would be tacky in my pink room) and a huge field of gold with a few figures and some trees and maybe a pagoda or two on it, the screen could look gaudy—but it doesn't.

To the right of the screen hang six black-and-white photos in plain, almost invisible chrome frames. I say they're invisible frames because at one point in my life I would never have hung anything framed in chrome next to something gold. But in this case the chrome isn't noticeable, because it doesn't detract from the overall effect.

The thing I've learned about putting things together in a home is that the details don't matter nearly as much as you think they will. When rooms are the result of hours of conscious thought, they tend to be contrived and uncomfortable. What counts is a sense of order and an instinct about what works. The process of creating a nourishing environment probably starts when our mothers say they trust us. Sooner or later, we learn to trust ourselves.

The best thing, for example, about the combination of tall, Chinese screen and stark black-and-white photos is the strongly graphic shapes in both the photos and screen. The screen is elaborate and a trifle self-important with its sense of history; the photos are simple, both contemporary and very American in form. As in the perfect marriage, elements of each partner's personality balance those in the other.

In front of the space between the photos and the screen, and right next to the muted, print-covered chaise longue, are my pots. Two are large and black, with shapes as strong as the Mexican arms it took to mold the clay. One of them, the biggest of the three, is a pale, sandy earth color. It is a plain pot that took up the entire back seat of my small car when I bought it at a local Mexican crafts market, and in certain lights it almost glows. It is a perfect foil for the overstated gold background of the Chinese screen and the geometry of the six art prints. Like the con artist who marries a homebody, my belongings keep each other from sinking into predictability.

I think it has taken me all my life to see how these things could—and should—fit together. The pink room is an act of daring, if not downright defiance. The pots are my favorites, worth pennies but as visually exciting as Technicolor dreams. The screen is so gorgeous it's excessive. The photos are our joint treasures, one taken by Andre Kertesz and the rest by my husband. The pink-and-blue print on the chaise sort of blends in. I love its muted geometry. My husband no longer hates it, but is still irritated that I didn't seek his opinion before ordering a major piece of furniture covered in it. Everything on or near that wall is a risk.

Until I sat down to think about it, I didn't realize that our homes give us great satisfaction for reasons other than that they are nice backdrops for life. In a way, they *are* life, canvases that help us record our achievements at least as much as paychecks—and in ways far less mercenary:

• Our homes encourage us to develop a distinctive style. I love antiques, all things Mexican and beautiful, rich fabrics. I have learned a fair amount about all these things, beginning when I bought yardage of a beautiful fabric I couldn't live without and stored it away until the right time.

• Our homes reflect various stages we move through as we move toward the elusive goal of maturity. Growing up. Wisdom that comes with experience. A look back on your domestic history should show you things about yourself you may still not know.

• We learn about trying and failing in our homes. Taking risks. Reinventing our notions of home. Mastery. I see women decorate their apartments and homes in tight little formulas. Peach and white, and everything shiny and new. They won't take risks, unless the current magazines okay it. Not even a dash of hot turquoise. Boring.

Years ago, I could not have designed this room as I have, and I would have been embarrassed to admit how much pleasure it gives me. "It's not rocket science," I might have said. But it is definition. Invention. Growth.

Self-Reliance

JANICE ROSENBERG

When the last shelf is in place, I stand back to admire my work. Instead of six warped wooden boards set at irregular intervals, the narrow closet in my new kitchen now has five white vinyl-covered steel-wire shelves. This satisfying transformation is the result of an entire afternoon spent sawing, drilling, and hammering. My shoulder aches from battling the hacksaw. The palm of my right hand tingles where the screwdriver handle raised a blister and then rubbed it raw. My navy turtleneck is white with plaster dust and I don't smell sweet, but seeing what I've accomplished inside this closet makes up for all of that. When I was a kid, girls weren't supposed to do these kinds of things.

On Sunday afternoons when I was six or seven, my father sat for hours with my older brother, teaching him to use his Erector set. It came with enough miniature steel beams to build a model of the Brooklyn Bridge, plus a real electric motor to which pulleys could be attached. I had studied simple machines in first grade, so I knew what pulleys did.

My brother didn't know a pulley from an inclined plane—and he didn't care. He longed to be out playing football with his pals. I watched enviously as he struggled to keep the tip of the screwdriver in the slot of a tiny screw, struggled to pick up a minute nut with his clumsy fingers. *I can do it*, I wanted to shout. *Let me do it*. But my father preferred torturing his uninspired son to working with his curious daughter.

About that time I was given a plastic spool with four sprockets, on which I crocheted a long rope of multicolored yarn. I meant to coil it into a full-sized rug, but boredom kept it down to dollhouse size. That same year I wove countless potholders from elastic loops of cloth on a one-square loom. When I was eight my mother taught me how to knit. Together we sewed doll clothes and baked cookies. I liked all these crafts, but none of them offered the challenge that mechanical devices did.

When I was nine, I followed a diagram in my science book and built a telegraph powered by a dry-cell battery. There were no instructions, just a diagram. I didn't ask my father for help. I wrapped a nail with insulated wire for the electromagnet and cut a strip of metal from an empty can for the sending key. Fearlessly, I hooked it up and thrilled to the short-long taps I sent in my private version of Morse code.

The next day several boys brought similar home-built models to school. I was angry with myself for leaving mine at home. No one would be impressed by it the next day. At the same time, I knew I had not brought it because girls didn't do that kind of thing. I grew up with that contradiction: girls didn't do those kinds of things, but I did. When I was twelve I found the Erector set in the basement and built myself a motor-driven elevator. I took it apart and built a drawbridge, took that apart and built a crane, and took that apart and built a giant vehicle I designed. Then, satisfied that I could do it on my own, I took it apart and put the set back in the basement without bothering to display my work.

Throughout my childhood I watched my father fix things. He could stop the screen door from slamming, change the rubber drive belt on the vacuum cleaner and rewire a lamp. By the time I was in high school, I had taken over many of his chores without consulting him. I put together those frustrating unassembled toys for my younger brother. I threaded the movie projector. I repaired loose doorknobs, having determined on my own that a tiny screw on the doorknob shank controlled the mechanism.

I took my reputation for being handy with me when I married. My skill at operating an electric drill impressed my husband. His father could barely change a fuse; his mother had so much trouble inserting the beaters in her electric mixer that she went back to her trusty eggbeater. During our first year together I put up curtain rods and unjammed the garbage disposer. When I showed my husband how to wire his stereo, he said, completely serious, "I didn't know that girls could do these things."

Like me, he'd been brought up to think that girls turned into mothers and teachers, not auto mechanics or surgeons like my father. When women's liberation and ERA came along, I thought of those Erector-set Sundays and blamed my father for leaving me without a profession. I blamed him for not encouraging me, for seeing gender instead of aptitude. "If only he had let me . . ." I would think. "If only he had shown me . . ." I would say. "Look, I have his nimble fingers, his perfectionist's eye. I could have been a surgeon just like him."

I spent the next few years resenting him, thinking with bitterness that he had gotten what he deserved. Neither of my brothers followed his example. Neither had the talents that I'd inherited. What irony! My father never had the chance to say the words "my son, the doctor." But it wouldn't have meant a thing to him to say those same proud words about a girl.

I give my work on the closet a final, critical look. One shelf slants slightly downward to the left. Here and there an anchor rides above the surface of the wall. Pencil markings mar the new white paint. But these mistakes don't spoil the closet as a whole. Tough, efficient, practical, expressing my self-reliance and resourcefulness, this closet will make me proud for years. And as if all that were not enough, I see it as a further proof that my father did not know what girls could do.

A week later I invite my parents over. When we're all standing in the kitchen my son opens the closet door. "See what my mom did, Grandpa?" he says.

Before he can question anything, I point a defiant finger at the shelving. "I fitted in five shelves where there used to be just four. I had to cut the darn things with a hacksaw. Did you ever do that? It makes a sound like ten sets of fingernails scraping blackboards. I had to drill four holes for each shelf and put in anchors. See?" I hold out my palm to show him my still-healing sore. "I got this from the screwdriver."

He steps up close, his back to me, and presses one hand hard against a shelf. "Sturdy," he says as he continues to examine my work. I see his finger slide over an unused, uncorrected hole I had drilled too low for the top shelf.

To distract him from my error I say, "When I was little I wanted to be a carpenter." Although it's true, I have never admitted it to anyone before.

He turns around and smiles at me, a proud and slightly sheepish grin. To my surprise, he says, "You could have done it, too." He takes another long look at my hand and then pats my shoulder. "Next time buy yourself a pair of work gloves."

"Now that you mention it," I say, "there's another project

that I have in mind. It's in the upstairs bathroom. Would you take a look? I could use your expertise."

As we go upstairs together, two grown-ups who can make mistakes, I finally forgive him for his shortsightedness. Girls can't do things like that, I think, but women can.

Spaces

LAURA GREEN

When I was pregnant with my second child and outgrowing my surroundings as well as my body, my husband and I went house hunting. We wanted a house in the city, in a neighborhood that would reassure us that we were still hip even though we were parents. That house was unaffordable. Instead, we bought a big old apartment filled with promise in a neighborhood on the verge of regentrification. It was an answer to our prayers.

But it was like all answered prayers. We had to learn to live with what we thought we wanted. Since the area was run-down, the apartment was a steal. It was underpriced by nearly 50 percent and solid as a rock. There were problems; I guess that goes without saying. The former owners had milked the building, leaving the new condo owners—eighty of us—to deal with the serious problems of leaky roofs and a temperamental boiler and the lesser evils of quarter-sized water bugs that roamed the range, the floors, even the beds at midnight.

The apartment's walls were painted every color of mustard, from Dijon to ballpark. The fireplace had been partially sealed up and decorated with brown bathroom tile stuck on with glue that could and did burn. A sunny ell off the living room had been walled up to make another bedroom. The kitchen was designed for the stylish young couple of 1880 who never did anything so menial as cook their own food. Designed for expendable servants to swelter in, it was cramped and tiny. The refrigerator was at the end of a hallway by the back door so the iceman could deliver ice for the icebox. Once I said I wanted to tear down a wall to make room for a refrigerator near the stove, I realized I was talking contractors, if not an architect. From that point, there was no turning back. We had become rehabbers.

From the beginning, my husband and I had been itching to fix up something, to put our mark on a place. We were as territorial as animals—for the same essential reason. We were nesting and raising a new generation.

The summer before we got married, we took a few weeks off to go camping in Ontario. When we weren't huddled in the cold in our tiny tent in the woods, half drunk on the sight and sound and taste of each other, we were driving through an austere countryside dotted with iris-filled meadows, abandoned farms, and struggling, isolated north-woods towns. When we got to a town, we would drive up the side streets, admiring the old Victorian houses. Though each house was different, our conversations ran the same course. If the houses were ours, we would build a greenhouse, get rid of tiny rooms, and redo the kitchen. But that was all we agreed on, house after house, town after town, trip after trip. Then we started squabbling. He talked about decks and a hot tub. I said they would ruin the look of a place. I wanted skylights. He argued that they would leak and get dirty.

I should have known then that we would get married, that it was just a matter of time for a couple who daydreamed about tearing out parlors and putting in kitchens. And I should have realized that we would fight about a lot of things, not just windows and walls.

But blessed with innocence, we never discussed how we wanted to live. We didn't understand each other and we couldn't comprehend the real issue of remodeling. Cheesy pipes and cost overruns aren't what get you. No, the problem with remodeling is getting what you paid for only to find out that it isn't what you wanted after all.

A few months after that trip we were married and I was pregnant. Not long after that, I was pregnant again and we were looking for a place for a family of four. When we bought the apartment, the bank gave us enough money to play out the final act of a romance with all things hypermodern that began when I was in college and put the obligatory Mondrian poster on my dorm room wall. In a desire to get rid of clutter and dramatize the big old rooms, we stripped our turn-of-the-century apartment of every inessential wall, door, and room. We designed a space that was as loftlike and open as you could get in an eight-room apartment. We tore out a few rooms to make a big kitchen that fed into a dining room, which opened into a living room, which led to a library and a bedroom. Anyone with a sense of privacy would have been appalled.

The fact that we overdid the openness went unnoticed at first because the apartment looked grand. Unimpeded by shades, the sun poured in the wide windows and made our bare wooden floors glow like old money. Without much to distract the eye, the architectural details on the all-white walls and ceilings stood out dramatically. The living room had one couch, a pile of cushions, and some geometric foam shapes. One of my best friends insisted on calling it dope-smoking furniture even though we were settled down and straight as Mormons. If you didn't get the couch, you wouldn't get comfortable—but even as you fidgeted, you couldn't help but notice the space.

Once we cluttered up the place with people, though, the drawbacks of Spartan design became apparent. It was terribly noisy. The baby's cries bounced off those hard walls and reverberated in my head. My daughter's Big Wheel sounded like a garbage truck on the bare floor. The stereo throbbed like a jungle drum.

Our open floor plan killed any natural privacy. Given the lack of intimacy that followed the birth of another baby, the design of the apartment dealt a few body blows to what was, at the time, a rocky marriage. Finding a place to argue our differences was difficult. Because sound bounced off those uncluttered walls like a racquetball, we tried to squabble sotto voce, but that made us feel silly. We rarely resolved anything. As soon as we started shouting, a small child with big, worried eyes would appear in one doorless doorway or another, anxious to be reassured. While I was comforting, my husband either fell asleep or hightailed it downstairs to the communal patio. Arguing there was out of the question because it was the village square and everyone would discuss our business, with or without us.

But even if it wasn't ideal for us, the apartment was a good place for little children. Since sound carried easily from room to room, a cry for help never went unheard. The wooden living-room floors were perfect for roller skating, which the kids did one endless Chicago winter when the snow piled up outside and the temperature stayed below freezing for weeks on end. That cursed foam furniture held up to playing and made great castles and forts.

In time, we tempered the place. Toys added grace notes. Nicks and crayon marks on the walls humanized it. The desks in the kitchen and the dining room gave it a reassuring, slovenly human touch.

The place changed us about as much as we changed it. With a big kitchen and two small children, I stayed home and cooked on weekends. Friends came in; we didn't go out. We had room for guests in our little fishbowl of a library. To give them a shred of privacy, we hung a sheet across the doorway. It looked as though we were getting ready to show home movies and reminded me of those beaded curtains in sultry silent films, but it worked.

Five years ago, for a variety of reasons (mostly financial), we put the apartment on the market, took our profit, and sank it into an old Victorian farmhouse in the burbs. It didn't look much different from the Canadian houses we had admired a decade earlier. But it is different from the apartment. As a result of 120 years of dogged remodeling by owners with more energy than sense, we live in a jumble of warrens and nooks thrown together like building blocks. Our bedroom has a half-hidden ell, as does the library, a nook where the children sprawl out on a padded bin left over from the old days. Scrunched up under an afghan, they can hear what is going on without being seen, a delicious prospect. There are corners for studying, old beds under old eaves. We have to make a point of finding each other.

We've done what we had to do, replacing disintegrating bathrooms, peeling off funky, fusty wallpaper, and fixing the leaky roof. We have an attic that you can't get to except by ladder, so installing skylights is out of the question. There's a slab for a greenhouse; the former owner had one but took it down because he said the plants were taking over his life. My husband is eyeing the space for a hot tub but we'll never put it in. We learned the basic remodeling lesson—live in a place, get the feel of it, then make changes only if you must.

Still, we're living in another answered prayer. We paid for Victorian charm and got the vicissitudes of Victorian living— poor wiring, narrow halls, tiny rooms, and one sloping up-stairs floor, a reminder of a remodeling project that took out one wall too many.

Like the apartment, the house has changed us. This kitchen doesn't encourage cooking, which gives me the excuse I need to stay out of it. Since the house has nine flower beds, I have instead become a somewhat reluctant gardener who digs in the spring, ignores in the summer, and curses in the fall.

But we have molded our lives, too, by our choice of home. During our everybody-into-the-pool years, our fishbowl ac-commodated the tumble and squeal of small children. When our need for peace and quiet became acute, we found a sanctuary from lives that are increasingly complex. We have a hideout for sitting and thinking, pastimes we once found utterly alien.

The good part about living in an answered prayer is that even if you only guess half right, you like much of what you get.

Old Tools

CARROLL STONER

It came to me one recent morning while I was making pancakes. Ideally, I realized, by the twentieth (not to mention the two hundredth) time you make the same meal, you should have a routine. If you're doing it right, making pancakes takes a few quick steps that hardly require thinking. Ideally.

It should work something like this: You grab your griddle— the one that's seasoned perfectly from years of use—and start heating it on your stove. You then toss the ingredients into the bowl you use for almost everything, so you can easily judge how many or how few pancakes you want to make. You mix the batter with a large spoon that can double as a measuring ladle so your pancakes come out the same size and flip them with a favorite spatula that behaves exactly as you tell it to. Ideally.

Instead of anything resembling a formula, though, I pull out my old frying pan, which was once Teflon-coated. The handle broke off years ago, and its sides are about two-inches high, so it's far from ideal; the height of the rim makes it difficult to get the spatula under each pancake.

I reach for a bowl and find a favorite—a heavy, deep-blue ceramic bowl at least fifty years old that I bought while shopping with a friend in one of our favorite country antique shops. She died a few years ago, and when I'd finished grieving, I started laughing about how nakedly competitive and funny she was. Almost every time I use that bowl I remember how aggravated she was not to have seen it first. ("Where did you get that bowl? I didn't see it," she said. Then came the charm. "I'm the one who collects bowls, you know," she said with a smile. Nice try, I thought.)

Then I reach for a spatula and find the one I use, the one with the missing rivet that causes the spatula part to rotate on its remaining rivet, making flipping pancakes—or anything, for that matter—unpredictable. To pour the batter into the pan, I grab a soup ladle and reflect on my mother's pancakes (all the same size and perfectly brown on both sides) and mine (frequently oddly shaped, messy little things).

We eat pancakes and bacon with warmed syrup and butter for breakfast. No one cares that they aren't perfect pancakes. Including me. Later, over coffee with my husband, I muse aloud that my pancake-making equipment leaves a lot to be desired. "How could I get this far in life and not have a routine for making pancakes?" I wonder.

To my surprise, he understands exactly what I mean. In fact, he gives the syndrome a name: Old Tools. "Every man would understand what you're saying," he says. You need old tools that you're familiar with, that feel right in your hand when you use them, and that have a specific purpose and use.

Old Tools. Some tools are specific, like a garlic press, or a brioche pan, or the pig platter I use for serving ham. Many more, though, are general, and should function as well for one chore as for others. But some of my most basic utensils are tools I bought before I realized how essential they would be. I think that crummy, broken spatula is a holdover from my single days, when I bought my first assortment of kitchen tools at a Macy's Dollar Days housewares sale.

The spatula should be replaced; I like my broken pan, though. It's an old friend. Even if it doesn't work for pancakes because of its high, right-angled rim, it's fine for pepper steak and perfect for pork chops. The country-kitchen blue bowl is a beauty, even though it weighs about five pounds and is too heavy to be used for pouring pancake batter into a pan. If I do use it, I'll need the perfect pancake-dipping spoon, big enough to make pancakes worth eating, small enough to be . . . exactly the right size.

If I were a carpenter, my tools would be the best I could afford. It's impossible, I believe, to buy a hammer that's as cheap and fragile as many kitchen tools. I am, among other things, a cook and a baker, and I need well-made tools that will last a long time.

One reason for the existence of junky kitchenware is our attitude about domestic work. Fine carpentry tools exist because men think enough of their tools and their tasks to be willing to pay the price for good ones. When a carpenter—or a homemaker—reaches for a tool, it should be reliable, sturdy, and appropriate for its use. Think like a tradesman, or like an apprentice chef, who buys one good knife a year as his budget allows. If you want to become an expert homemaker, consider yourself an apprentice for the first years.

Ultimately, by the time you can call yourself a master, you should have tools that are worthy of your trade. Old Tools.

Recidivism

Laura Green

The annual pre-preschool conference was held the week after I told the principal that we would be sending our daughter to another school for junior kindergarten. I mention this because after all these years, I think my announcement was the reason the teacher laid into me.

"Laura," she said, leaning toward me like a heat-seeking missile homing in on a jet fighter, "do you ever read to your child?"

Yes, I said. Yes, I did.

"Your daughter seems neglected," she told me. "With your, uh, work and the baby, are you remembering to spend time with her?"

"Yes, yes, I am," I believe I mumbled, trying to breathe in and out regularly so she could not see the pain she had caused me. I do not remember the rest of our conversation. I just wanted to get out of there without her seeing my tears.

I have always been vulnerable to the charge that I am not a good enough mother. Like every working mother, I sometimes wonder if my loyalties are too divided, if I shouldn't try harder, give more of myself. My working life has been a crazy quilt of full-time jobs, part-time jobs, leaves of absence, no jobs, and freelancing. Mine has been the on-again, off-again career of a woman who needs to be two places at once.

Still, my children are fine, and when they are not fine they do well enough. They talk on the phone, interrupt, jump up and down, preen in the mirror, struggle with homework, snuggle, tell jokes, fight, act silly, swear, talk with their mouths full, stick up for other kids, kiss us and hug us and do all the other things that normal, giddy, full-of-life children do. They are not damaged, as far as I can tell, by not having me around every day, year-in, year-out. However, I am a child of the fifties, so that day I walked home from the nursery school, put the children down for their naps, and stuffed my head in the pillow and wept.

The fifties and their values. I hate them. I love them.

Much of fifties life was hunkered-down and closed-minded, and its lessons were clear. The fifties were nothing if not clear. As a result, rebellion was easy and safe. You were daring for saying damn. You could make a statement by wearing a black turtleneck. You didn't do drugs because there weren't any. There wasn't much sex, either. Other than tempting fate by getting into a car and tear-assing down a back road, it was possible to be a rebel with barely a physical or psychic scratch. It did us much more good than harm.

I could loathe the fifties if they were all bad—but they weren't. Everyone believed in the sacredness of the family— every family—and while that made life hard for those who weren't married or didn't have children, it was comforting to live that way. We ate dinner at six sharp every night, all of us at the table. Schools didn't dare schedule events during the dinner hour. No one would come. In the fifties, tradition was respected. My family was close enough to the old country to know its broken ties and the need to form new traditions. My grandmother and aunt came over for dinner on Friday nights. We ate in the dining room on the good dishes and everyone dressed nicely. I learned a lot about family history at those dinners.

If that was the up side of home life in the fifties, the down side was a woman's relationship with her home. Where women were concerned, the fifties were especially clear. Women didn't work outside the home. They held themselves back and raised their kids. They poured themselves into us with breathtaking commitment, transmuting their hopes for themselves into our little lives. Our accomplishments replaced theirs; their college diplomas went into the drawer and our report cards, puny substitutes, went onto the refrigerator.

It is seductive to think that if we just turned all our energy toward our children and their surroundings, they would turn out perfect and we would be perfectly happy in the reflected glow of their accomplishments. We would live for others and through them in a saintly sort of sacrifice. It would be such a relief to stop putting ourselves on the line. I think about that on days when work gets overwhelmingly hard. It would be so easy, I think, just to go home.

I could understand the allure of the fifties if its values were the only ones I learned, but they weren't. My mother was a tough-minded union organizer, which utterly bewildered the stay-at-home wives of the self-made businessmen in our neighborhood. My mother disdained most of these women because they didn't do anything. But I liked them. They were my friends' mothers, nice ladies who made me sandwiches when I went to their houses after school. There was something reassuring about a mother in an apron in the kitchen.

We were different—a little more unpolished and a lot more interesting. Our house didn't have the attention to detail you find when a woman makes her home the center of her life. Instead, it was a casual mess of furniture with a carpet that was downright scruffy. Nothing matched. Most of the decorations, if you could call them that, came from a client of my father's. I'm not sure what he did for a living, but he paid his legal bills in lamp bases and ashtrays as big as hats. The living room lamps were incised with fake Cro-Magnon cave paintings, and I could look up from my homework and watch cave men chase wooly mammoths around the lamps.

In contrast, our neighbors decorated their living rooms with brocade-covered furniture and formal family portraits. Their homes were neutral, careful, dull. Nothing much happened there. Our house was hardly ever quiet. When I came home, someone was always in the middle of a passionate discussion. It was what home ought to be in the ways that count, but I didn't appreciate that until much, much later. What I knew was that we were unusual and that I didn't want to be.

Not unreasonably, my mother assumed my sister and I would be like her, not like the other mothers. She wanted us to be good wives, good mothers, and successful professionals, though she wasn't particular about the order. My father, who was much less conservative than his gray suits and quiet voice let on, thought I should become a commercial artist. That way, he said, I could always find work in any big city. He must have known even then that I would leave the neighborhood one day. Under their tutelage, we didn't do half bad; but in the short run, I just wanted a fifties family like everyone else's.

I drove my mother crazy. She was struggling with real adversaries. She wanted me to understand that her work was significant, that it mattered, that she mattered. I wanted her to come home and redo the living room with that shag carpeting that crept over the neighbors' floors like crabgrass. What can I say? For me it was not a question of values but of toss pillows. I wanted my mother to quit work, come home, and bake me some cookies. Then I wanted her to iron my father's shirts. That was what women were supposed to do.

Eventually I grew beyond the neighborhood. I went to high school, made new friends, and switched from Peter Pan collars to turtlenecks. We had a lot of fun putting down the smug excess of my neighbors. We proclaimed our allegiance to art and creativity and took turns modeling naked for each other.

I moved away as soon as I could, but I am forever measuring myself by home's standards, even when they no longer apply. One of my old friends used to know Bernardine Dorhn. He said it was easy to pick her out in a gathering of Weathermen because she was the only one who never put her elbows on the table when she ate. She was back in the neighborhood.

I am stuck with my legacy of the fifties, the good and the bad. I love being surrounded by family, and now that I live near my sister, the closeness is even better than I remember. The rest of the fifties are what dogs me—that women's magazine ethic that permeated life back then, the recidivists who would call me a better woman if I never left the house. The call for mothers to go home again and give up what they barely have a grip on is so seductive. It would be so easy. So safe. So treacherous.

BOUND
FOR HOME

Other People's Houses

The houses I love are so unlike my own.

I love houses that have the flotsam and jetsam of well-lived lives trailing from every surface. I love houses that have phone numbers and children's heights written on the walls, and heaps of seashells on the window sills, and skis stuck in the corner and ironing boards open in the kitchen. I love houses with crazy hats hanging from a hat stand, and cupids painted above the bathroom sink, and wisps of crepe paper peeping from behind thumbtacks stuck in the walls, and pineapple tops growing in saucers.

You can go through a whole lifetime without seeing more than one or two such houses. In my lifetime, I've known two. One belongs to an artist, the other to a Lutheran minister's wife. (The artist is married to a writer, and the minister's wife is married to the minister, but I think of the houses as belonging to the women.)

The artist's kitchen has messages from friends written on the wall by the big wood stove where she bakes bread daily. Her living room has fabrics she loves permanently pinned to the furniture with straight pins (although when she discovered the glue gun she was quick to see its uses for upholstering). She has pots of red geraniums on an ironing board stuck behind a Victorian settee, and she sets the table with odd china she's bought for its color. The bathroom is papered with

maps scotch-taped together and brown with age and has a tiny
loft for reading that she and her husband made for their
daughter. That daughter is now in her thirties and long gone,
but the hiding place is still in the bathroom. That's characteristic of such houses. They are like things from the sea, covered
with barnacles and limpets.

One day the artist visited me in my own house and took a
fancy to a bedspread in my guest room. "I'll make you a rug to
match!" she said. Fifteen minutes later we were at the hard-
ware store buying paints. Three hours later, she rose from her
knees and said, "There!" Around the periphery of the room
was a three-foot-wide border made of the same design elements as the bedspread and in the same colors. On that same
visit, as we walked through my garden she told me the secret
of the prettiest nosegays: put them in a vase just the way you
gather them.

The Lutheran minister's wife's house doesn't reveal the same
eye for color that the artist's shows everywhere, even on the
dashboard of her car, without even being conscious of it. But
it has the same air of rampant creativity and of something
else—an energy that even the artist's house doesn't approach.

The first time I visited, I stood stock still, rendered motion-
less and speechless by sensory bombardment. Laundry heaped
upon the dining room table, spilled to the floor, trailed across
the carpet, and rose onto another chair. Children were jumping rhythmically up and down on the sofa, still holding toast
from breakfast. A sewing machine was set up on the dining
room table, where a sewing project—sixteen pairs of drapes
for a neighbor's house—was in full sway. The floor was so
littered with children's toys that I had to pick my way across.
In the kitchen, twenty quarts of green beans sat cooling on the
table, and on the sideboard half a dozen flowers were being
pressed. My friend made no apologies—no small act of courage when you're the minister's wife.

While I waited as she answered the phone, her five-year-old
son asked if I would like him to make me a snake. He took a

piece of fabric from the scraps at hand, folded it wrong side
out, and sewed three sides of it on his mother's fancy, top-of-
the-line foreign sewing machine. He then turned it right side
out, stuffed it with cotton batting, cut a snippet of red felt,
stuck it in as a tongue, sewed it up, and presented it to me.
His seven-year-old sister, not to be outdone, went to get the
quilt she was working on. I am no judge of quilts, but it
appeared to me to be the equivalent of any adult quilt I have
ever seen in the complexity of the pattern and the perfection of
the workmanship.

There's no company cleanup or company manners or company anything else in such houses, and yet you feel more
honored, more privileged to be present than in any other
house. What you see is what you get—and what you get is the
real person.

Nothing is sacred in such houses. There are treasured objects, to be sure; nothing is ever thrown away because the
owners have a fierce, almost mystical, attachment to objects.
But the house itself is not sacrosanct. No one worries about
whether the value of the house will go down if a door is cut in
a wall.

There's often a lot of unfinished work visible in such houses—
quilts that were never completed, pictures that were never
matted, additions that are still being worked on three years
later—because the kind of people who live in such houses care
more about the process than the product.

The overwhelming feeling such houses give is a feeling of
richness. They are the opposite of all that's niggardly and
careful and calculating. They impart the joyous, generous
sense of there being lots and lots and lots more where that
came from.

Although you may love such houses, as I do, you can't
decide to have one. It either happens, because you're that sort
of a person, or it doesn't. Most of us need more order and
control—we're too fragile, too afraid that all those things

unfinished and things undone and things revealed will take over, swamping us.

And the truth of the matter is, most of us don't want that kind of a house. We want a house that reflects the kind of person we are trying to become. The houses I love reflect the owner as she is or was, wherein lies their power.

Motel Life

LAURIE ABRAHAM

I lived about a quarter mile from the beach, just down the road from the Jolly Roger Motel. It never occurred to me that I should not be living there at the age of twenty, or that I should not share a bedroom with a man I had only known for a year and not well at that, a man who was widely perceived as my rival in journalism school. I don't think it occurred to Jonathan either, or perhaps any doubts he had about living with me were outweighed by his need to live cheaply. I had forgotten how much we paid for our efficiency at the Anchor. Jonathan says he never will: $320 a month split two ways, payable to the ever watchful landlady, Ernestine Richter.

But I'm getting ahead of myself. First, let me make it clear that Jonathan and I were not lovers. (To anyone who knows us from college, that can be classified as an absurd understatement.) We slept three feet apart in narrow twin beds, under thin pink floral covers. A small nightstand and lamp were all that came between us—in a physical sense, at least. It was autumn and we were in Fort Lauderdale, Florida, for our first important internship, at the *Miami Herald*—easily the most prestigious paper in our university's program. Jonathan and I had what it took to get the nod: big aspirations, some talent, and an immature obsession with being better than everyone else.

Back then, where I lived and who I lived with seemed irrelevant. If I had a dream home, it was a grimy apartment that would prove that my work was my life. I assumed everything would fall into place when I had the career I wanted, and the first step to that career was my internship. It was up to students to find their own accommodation. Several of my classmates had talked about applying to certain newspapers because they had a relative in town or some other convenient, affordable place in which to stay. Not I. I drove south from Cleveland, Ohio, in my father's Cutlass, with no idea where I would live.

At first, the one-story compound of efficiency apartments did not seem so bad. It was made up of two rows of off-white stucco units, divided by a narrow strip of crab grass infested with chameleons. *The Anchor* was emblazoned across the front in tired blue, underlined by a large piece of driftwood. Jonathan and I had surveyed this much when our landlady-to-be, Ernestine, approached in her white sedan. Ernestine had limp bleached hair and wore spike heels. Her eyes were skeptical: she seemed to think Jonathan and I might upset the predictable bonhomie of the Anchor's winter residents, which included a few old French Canadian men, some transients, and a kind but wary woman who'd spent her younger days in New Jersey. I know Ernestine assumed that Jonathan and I pushed our single beds together, and she probably feared that our screams of passion would interrupt the slumber of the regulars. Instead, the regulars woke me, opening and shutting doors, banging pans, and bellowing in French at 7 A.M.

Privacy was not easy to come by at the Anchor. But it had not been something I wanted. During my first two years in college I shared a room with a woman who remains one of my closest friends; I had come to believe that even bad companionship was better than none at all. What I did not take into account were the nights that I would spend lying stiffly in my bed, a few feet from Jonathan, wiping away an occasional tear. Frustration at work, loneliness—I don't remember exactly why I was upset. What I do remember is Jonathan's breathing: he was right there, his chest rising and falling. I did not dare cry.

It was uncomfortable to be so close to Jonathan in body but so far from him in spirit, although at the time I did not recognize that. We each took our turns in the shower, steps away from where the other slept. He wore powder-blue pajamas to bed; I wore T-shirts. I did not guard myself. When my boyfriend came to visit at the end of my internship, he was furious to learn that I had been sleeping in the same room as Jonathan—and in a T-shirt, no less. Paul could not believe that it had never occurred to me to tell him. He fantasized about women while he walked along the street, sat in class, and debated the value of the post-modern aesthetic, and so he imagined the room Jonathan and I shared sparking with sexual tension. But the only thing that ever charged the air between Jonathan and me was occasional resentment.

My best friend, Lisa, with whom I live now, tells me she thought I was daft to imagine that Jonathan and I could get on in such close quarters. Even at that age, she was better at providing for her home life than I was. One night soon after I had moved in with him, I called her from a gas-station pay phone. (Phones were too expensive for us.) I was desperate; Jonathan and I had been grocery shopping. We had planned to split the cost of items we both used, but when I suggested a liter of Coke, Jonathan balked. "Powdered drinks are cheaper," he told me. "You don't have to pay for water."

What I wanted most in Fort Lauderdale was not privacy but easy companionship. After the Anchor's morning melee, residents locked themselves in air-conditioned apartments. (We, of course, could not afford to turn ours on.) On my days off, I slept as late as possible to avoid the empty day that lay before

me. Out of bed by about 10 A.M., I'd cross from the linoleum-
floored bedroom to the living room/kitchen, which was covered in threadbare green. On good days, I remembered to
avoid the burrs that clung to the carpet. Breakfast was raisin
bran in a pea-green plastic bowl accompanied by "The Wheel
of Fortune." For a while, I ran in the mornings, down the hot
asphalt side streets to A1A, the main drag in Fort Lauderdale.
Or I'd go to the beach to read. I took to escaping on weekends,
to my aunt's house near Palm Beach, to Lisa's place six hours
north in Jacksonville. My best times were spent there. Lisa's
uncle had turned over his comfortable apartment to her and
Sandy, another college friend. I recall one night in particular:
Lisa's uncle made homemade spaghetti sauce, and the four of
us sat around eating, drinking red wine, and smoking dope.
The room crackled with the warmth I missed in Fort Lauderdale.

I talked to Jonathan before I wrote this piece, and I find it
hard to believe that there was such animus between us. Indeed, he reminded me of an incident I had forgotten, one that
shows how estranged we were. On Thanksgiving that year, I
worked all day and then drove an hour north to my aunt's
house for dinner. I did not invite Jonathan. I would like to
think he would not have accepted, although I am probably
rationalizing. So he ate the "turkey special" alone at Howard
Johnson's. He told me afterward that all the tables in the
restaurant were lined up so that the diners faced the ocean. It
was pouring rain; they had nothing—or more precisely,
nobody—else to face.

I like to think that I now choose the place and person I live
with more carefully, but a part of me continues to disdain the
importance of home. I'm still emerging from the "I'll live in a
garret; just give me the right job" stage. If I had been wiser
that fall, if I had known myself well enough to get my own
apartment or at least my own room, maybe Jonathan and I
would have been able to maintain a friendly rivalry. We had
that potential. Every once in a while, when we escaped the
false intimacy of the Anchor and the tension of the office, we

played a little. Like the night we drank whiskey sours from plastic cups at the Jolly Roger. We sat at the piano bar from dusk until the moon shone; then Jonathan's liquor started talking and he asked our waitress for a date. She refused, but I don't think he cared that I saw that small defeat. We were commiserating about our jobs, talking and laughing. We appreciated each other for a few hours. If only we could have savored the evening later in the privacy of our own homes.

Table Talk

JANICE ROSENBERG

My father used dinnertime to get on my older brother's case. "Sit up straight," he would say. Or "Use a piece of bread to push your food onto your fork." Or "Can't you stop that coughing?" Sometimes my father quizzed him about his homework. "Did you study your spelling?" "What is the capital of Utah?" No one in our family lingered over dessert. I vowed that when I grew up I would never ruin family dinners by treating my kids that way.

We all know that some of life's best conversations happen over food. Since this is true with friends, why shouldn't it be true with children? But what was easy for me to achieve with a bunch of grown-ups didn't always come naturally to me at the family dinner table.

So I made some dinner table rules. We parents don't pull rank. We listen without interrupting and do our best to correct factual inaccuracies with kindness. The premise behind these rules is the old but wonderful rule "Treat your guests like family and your family like guests." A guest who spills her milk isn't called a careless idiot and sent from the table. A guest who confuses Senator Paul Simon with musician Paul Simon isn't confronted with hysterical laughter.

We have more specific rules, too. For the kids: no whining or standing on the chairs. For us: no nagging or criticism. For everyone: no reading or television. And recently we've started turning on our answering machine so we're not distracted by the phone. The kids aren't allowed to sculpt their bread, kick each other under the table, or make gagging noises over a fellow diner's preference for mayonnaise on roast beef sandwiches (although I know they still make silent retching motions behind my back).

It hasn't been easy. We endured the days of formula and mushy cereal. Then ketchup on the placemats and chocolate pudding in the kids' eyelashes distracted us from our efforts at decent conversation. Only gradually did talking begin to occupy more time than cleaning up. And when it finally did, finding subjects to keep us all interested was tricky. Years ago my mother had large dinner parties almost monthly. Her fear that conversation would run dry led her to make a list of possible topics, many suggested by articles in the *Reader's Digest*. She kept the list in a kitchen cabinet. When table talk lagged, she would excuse herself and come back with a question or opinion to start things rolling. "We have more trouble with our mail," she said one night as I helped serve. In the kitchen I scanned her list and found "Organizing the Paper in Your Life." When I heard her protest against a guest's complaint about the length of time it took air mail letters to arrive, I knew what her topic would be. "No, not that," my mother said. "I mean all the stuff you get every day. I heard about this wonderful new method of getting organized." And she was off and running.

Even though I know this activity will sound contrived and too much like my mother (and I don't like the invidious comparison), I make a point of watching the news for dinner table stories while I cook. My husband Michael listens to public radio on his drive home for the same reason. I told my family about car battery testing on frozen lakes near International Falls, Minnesota, even after they looked up from their pizza to see if I had lost my marbles. If a news story interests me, I consider that reason enough to repeat it. Weird as the stories sometimes sound, telling them is almost always better than asking, "Did you have a nice day?" or "How was the math test?" The first question can dead-end in yes or no; the second produces anxiety.

Our children have grown used to dinner subjects as varied as local politics, travel, and of course, personal family history. None of us has ever refrained from voicing an opinion, even if we don't know exactly what we're talking about. My husband's year-long search for an additional medical partner led to conversation about the kinds of people you like to work with and the kinds you don't. A school flyer on folk music took us from Bob Dylan through Woodie Guthrie, then on to spirituals and from there to South Africa. One evening over rib lamb chops, which I seldom serve because they're so expensive, I said that when I was a child we ate them once a week. My younger son commented on how my parents hate to see food wasted and we talked about the effects of living through the Depression.

My husband and I learned to listen carefully. My kids often approach personal subjects with phrases like "What if someone . . ." or "A friend of mine said . . ." or "I read in Dear Abby today . . ." We realized that the neutral territory of the third person gave them the freedom to tell us what was on their minds. We learned to watch for certain abstract phrases that meant something important was coming. We struggled to respond honestly—as we would with a friend—and without probing.

We learned not to expect miracles. Weeks have passed with nothing more enlightening under discussion than a review of the latest Steve Martin movie. After all these years I've learned there are necessary dry spells. Hard days at work or school, misunderstandings with friends—any of these things can make a person lose the will to socialize.

Yet years of trying to create conversation taught me something about silence. A couple of years ago when my older son's PSAT scores came back lower than he had hoped, he did not say a word at dinner. He and I happened to be eating alone that night. I felt like half of a blind date, tossing out topics that might catch his interest. Were the Bulls likely to win the game? How was the film society doing at school? Nothing helped. At the time I felt frustrated, defeated. But later I wondered if "nothing"—the nonjudgmental atmosphere created during better times—wasn't exactly what he needed.

International Children

CARROLL STONER

Once we spent six months planning a month-long vacation in France, where we rented and shared a house with another American family. That month altered our lives forever, providing us with experiences and a setting unlike anything we had ever known. When we returned we were a changed family.

To begin with, the house had no television, but it also had no living room. Life in the fifteenth century, when that section of the house was built, was lived in the dining room, with its huge fireplace, and on the porch overlooking the vineyards. No one over the centuries had felt any need to remodel or change the layout of the house, so it continued to dictate our way of life. Evenings were spent around the long, ageless table. That month surely gave rise to our present dining room, with its big, indestructible laminated table and its sofa and chest, filled with the craft materials, that have made the room a nerve center of our lives.

The kitchen sent us home to our own with an increased appreciation of technology. But the tiny French refrigerator and lack of storage cupboards also taught us much about the improved expectations for food when it is shopped for every day and prepared with friends.

"Jolie, eh?" said the butcher as he held up our roast for the other women in his store to admire. And admire they did, saying, "Ooo, la la." When we bought beef and the market woman cheerfully told us she'd included the herbs and spices for the "daube" she knew we were going to prepare, it was almost as shocking as it was satisfying. How better to understand the importance of daily pleasures to the French than to have them treat domestic decisions with such respect. Which is why, of course, they spend their lives around their tables and have elevated cooking to an art.

It was there, at the age of nine, that our son decided to master French. It was there that he accepted our lifelong permission to pursue his wanderlust. It was there in the romantic French countryside, living a somewhat routine day-to-day life, that we decided to add another child to our family, a decision that resulted in our daughter, born when I was thirty-seven and my husband was forty-seven. We were natural nesters, but domestic life abroad taught us much about the nesting potential at home.

Although I didn't know it for years after I began to travel, one of the best reasons to leave home is that it improves the quality of life when you return. As I grew more adept at living in other people's houses and countries, I learned much about the nature of domestic life at home.

It started when my father, who had dreams, gave me a

world guidebook. I was twelve and he was fifty-two. The thick paperback was published by Pan American Airlines back when they owned the world, and it was divided by country into categories of information, from "Climate" to "Common Courtesies and Local Customs." The book made an impression on me, because later when I was in my twenties and my father was a widower, we traveled together on the airline passes that came with my job, and he told me of his lifelong yearning to see the world. What surprised me even more than that was how at home he was wherever we went. I was in my early twenties when I learned this lesson from him: the rich aren't the only ones who are possessed of the confidence that makes them feel comfortable in any surroundings. He had it. I would have it. My children will have it.

What I want for my children is this: to feel comfortable enough in their own skins so that they can take that feeling with them wherever they go. I want them to become worldly and wise, though not cynical, about how the world works. I want them to travel far. And then I want them to come home again.

The best way to accomplish that, I know, is to push them from the nest at an early age. A study I read years ago sticks in my mind: Toddlers who are given lots of affection wander farther from their parents. Affection builds confidence. And in the way that people are never closer to their real selves than when they travel, new experiences are easier away from home. Which is a fine reason to travel in the first place. Which is a good reason to push your children out of the nest and into some life-broadening travel experiences. In the old days, those who could afford it "finished" abroad. My father had traveled widely. It showed.

My son never knew his grandfather, but they are alike—charming men who laugh softly and have easygoing personalities that don't hide their principles. My son, like my father, is at home in small Mexican towns, the kind with one cantina, a tortillería, and a church. Late at night and many years before my son was born, my father and I used to sit and drink tequila Mexican-style. He told me on one of those evenings that I could drink and drive like a man, his highest accolade, praise that still makes me laugh because of what it revealed about us. Sometimes he could be coaxed to sing, and when he did, he sang along with the Mexican bands without knowing the words, in the beautiful tenor voice that had made him a hit at family weddings and funerals. He was just as at home in fancy resorts, the kind where you sip drinks with flowers floating in them that cost ten times what it cost to belt down a shot at the cantina.

My son is as pragmatic as his grandfather. He's also blessed with perfect pitch and confesses that he sang and played for money on the streets of London and Strasbourg during a recent trip to Europe. But he didn't have to confess it; we already knew. He had saved his wages and we matched them and doled them out as needed, learning all about Western Union and American Express emergency funds as he went. The money didn't always arrive in time. Then the independence he yearned for became a harsh reality. Once, standing across the square from a French café with its lunch menu posted outside, he played and sang to raise enough money for that lunch, making his quota at the exact moment they closed their doors to prepare dinner.

I don't mind hearing of such misadventures because I remember the tough lessons I learned when I was young and intent on seeing the world. Living a life of forced idleness is the quickest way to learn how travel can cause a terrible vagueness, a reminder that living without structure is even more difficult than living with it. And being flat broke away from home brings with it a yearning and anxiety like no other. Then the journey becomes a burden—no fun and less adventure. At those times it feels wonderful to get home.

Money used to have everything to do with travel, but it doesn't any more. Wilbur and Orville Wright took care of that. But travel does have to do with children's concepts of the world at large and with their attitude toward comfort and necessity. Necessities at home are often luxuries in other parts of the world. Seeing that is good for everyone. Being worldly means being able to accept a certain random quality in life, and that begets openness and flexibility.

Remembering past trips and planning for future trips are almost equally satisfying. How luxurious to stop in the middle of a busy day, sit back, and think of returning to Pie de la Cuesta, a beach north of Acapulco. There we watched a glorious sunset while sipping tequila and seeing our young son jump through the wild surf for the sheer joy of leaping and running and flirting with danger. Another unforgettable part of that vacation was the ride back from the beach in a bus jammed with local families and their beach paraphernalia. The bus driver stopped at individual homes and at small roads leading to houses in the mountains, and we slowly wound our way back to the city. The ride, usually about fifteen minutes, took over an hour, but we didn't mind.

There was not a harsh word spoken during the hour on that crowded bus. It confirmed feelings about Indian ways—that they have a gentle acceptance very far from our need to control every part of life. No busful of North Americans could have been that peaceful.

We had never been so close to so many foreign families, and have never since been allowed such an intimate look into how they behave with each other. We were a family among families.

Stoops

LAURA GREEN

When I moved to Chicago, I lived in a neighborhood that was as densely packed as Paris and just as charming in its own solid, redbrick way. When I lived there, the rents were low; everyone was young and starting out, or old and in the last place they would live before the nursing home. I was drawn by the architecture, a confident hodgepodge of turrets, carvings, gargoyles, and bays. I loved the quirky front yards with English ivy and hosta spilling onto the brick walks and the sense of the past from the gas jets and wood paneling that remained in some of the converted parlors. The apartments were cramped, but they rarely stayed on the market more than a week because atmosphere, not space, was what my friends and I coveted. Instead of long living rooms we didn't have furniture for, we got original stained-glass windows, big cottonwoods that arched over the sidewalks, and front stoops.

If baseball is the American pastime, then "stoop-sitting," as they call it in Chicago, is the neighborhood pastime, a pleasure as simple as music. If there is one event, one tradition that turns a block into a community, sitting on the stoop is it.

On our block, stoop etiquette was as rigid as a tea ceremony. We met on one stoop only, the steep wooden steps of a woman who grew up in one of those tight xenophobic Chicago neighborhoods that gave birth to stoop-sitting as a balm for life in the factories and stockyards. Her house was on the east side of the street, where the stoop caught the late afternoon sun. Because she was the owner and not a tenant, it was okay for the rest of us to ease our tired hams on her wooden steps. We met there and nowhere else. We congregated only at certain times of the day and only if she was already there.

It would have been unthinkable to gather on Carol's stoop without Carol. We rarely went to Inge's, and we never met on Judy's porch or my porch, which lay in deep, cold, five o'clock shade. We weren't comfortable there. For one thing, my landlord sometimes sat at the grand piano in the first-floor bay window above our heads. Wearing only his boxer shorts, he banged out show tunes, as oblivious of us as we were aware of him. Even if he had been out in the garage puttering in his workshop, my landlady, a transplant from the suburbs, would have been uncomfortable with us. She was a nice person, but she observed what I have come to think of as suburban proprieties. We were expected to keep our distance. It would have been an invasion of her privacy for anyone, tenant or not, to sit on her front steps. She never would have called it a stoop; the idea of a stoop was alien to her.

Not to me. I took to stoop-sitting the way a small boy takes to dirt. I would have sat all day if I could, but that was out of the question. We never began before about 5 P.M., when everyone was returning to the block. The mothers who didn't work were finishing the rounds of kids' activities. The ones like me, who did work, were trudging home from the office. I collected the baby from the babysitter and often, without dropping my stuff off at my place (we lived on the third floor), plunked down on Carol's stoop to unwind and regroup.

Stoop-sitting is one of the few ways to bring the unhurried intimacy of domestic life outdoors. There's no hurry, no pressure to talk, no need to dress up. You just sit and drink your coffee, or read your mail, or balance your checkbook. You can be your unembellished self on someone's front stoop in the same way that you can be in your own living room.

Early evenings were for the women because we were the

first ones home. Carol and I sat in the late sun and had long, theoretical discussions about the psychology of raising children and the Freudian ebbing and flowing of our friends' lives. From time to time we would be interrupted by our neighbor down the street, who was in her mid-twenties and terribly earnest, a woman who boned up for dinner parties by reading the *New York Times*. "What do you think of intermediate-range missiles?" she would ask brightly, one or two toddlers clinging to her shorts. We thought she was a dolt, having mastered the art of dinner party discussions many years earlier.

Eventually we took the children home for dinner (something ethnic with lots of grains in it), then came back again with our coffee and our families. Conversationally, one of the great things about living in Chicago is its inescapable, Byzantine politics that reach right down to the street corner. Chicago politics is the one area where trickle-down theories produce floods of events. Its intricacy, its corruption, and its endless, awful local ramifications gave us plenty to talk about. As it grew darker and the fireflies came out, we nursed our coffee while the kids rode up and down the block on their tricycles, fell, bled, fought, giggled, got bitten by mosquitoes, and had a fine time.

Twelve years ago we had a second baby and moved to a bigger place on a busy street. There were no stoops worthy of the name, but the apartment complex had something almost as good—a communal yard with a redbrick patio, several picnic tables, and a few crusty grills. We must have looked crazy, grilling hamburgers a few steps from the traffic under the shadow of the curved high-rise across the street that looked like it belonged on a Caribbean beach. We gossiped, drank our beer, and ate our dinners in a fog of car exhaust as the kids wobbled by on their new two-wheelers.

The patio wasn't much different in spirit from Carol's stoop. We lived elbow to elbow and got to know one another in an extended-family, neighborhood way. When my son was a toddler, he called the place "my village." He got it right, the way kids do. The complex held four generations, including a handful of obdurate misanthropes and one or two nasty eccentrics who drew us together by being people nearly all of us could hate. All the place really needed to be like a village was a well, a few steep, cobbled streets, and three or four skulking dogs.

It has been years since I walked across the street to drink the last cup of coffee I would have on Carol's front stoop. The toddlers are now in high school. The crowd has scattered, to Florida, to Washington, to New York, split and re-formed through divorce and remarriage. Carol lives in another city house with steep front steps, but now she sits on her back porch, where she can be alone and enjoy her privacy. She is still my good friend, but it is just not the same when you have to meet in restaurants—as we did for breakfast for a full year after I moved away.

The sad truth is that none of us have much time for sitting on stoops, which takes an hour here and a half hour there if you're going to do it right. An indoor domestic life is all I can manage. Stoop life had time built into it for talk and for the quiet that lets bonds knit. When you invite people into your house, you have an obligation to entertain them, but sitting on a stoop is like pot luck. It just happens. It recharges the batteries in a more natural way than an evening dinner party and sends us home feeling connected to the human village, wherever it is, that our deepest memories come from.

I miss it.

Family Rituals

MARY BETH DANIELSON

Two curious things.

The first: a magazine report looks for the common denominator among National Merit Scholars. What the reporters discover is not common economic level among those children's families, not superior schooling, not a particular degree of either discipline or creativity in the home. What they find is that almost without exception, the brightest and most accomplished teenagers in this country come from homes where the family regularly sits down and eats supper together.

The second curious thing: a television talk show mentions that health professionals have noted a mysterious but direct correlation between good physical and mental health in children and those children having their own place at the family table.

This is fascinating stuff. Apparently familiarity and routine do not so much breed contempt as they breed bright, secure kids.

In college I knew a woman, Sammie, whose family dinnertime routine amazed me with its offhandedness. Every evening her mother made the dinner and put it on a warming platter on the kitchen counter. A few hours later she'd return, put the leftovers away, wash the bowl—and that was that. In between, family members who were hungry would help themselves to dinner and then rinse and plop their plate in the dishwasher.

Sammie was one of the sexiest and most sophisticated women I had met, which meant she really stood out at my conservative college. She had more makeup and toiletries than the rest of us put together and she knew how to use them. She wore hot pants while the rest of us wore A-line skirts. When 11:00 P.M. curfew came to our girls' dorm, she was right there, safely in her room. A few minutes later, she'd climb out her window to waiting lovers. She never got caught and she never got pregnant; her disdain for rules, learned at the kitchen counter, dazzled the rest of us.

Sammie earned a lot of A's in a lot of different classes, including physics and chemistry. But she also failed a fair number of courses, because her academic success depended on the state of her love life, which was rarely calm. By the end of our four years she had switched from a promising pre-med major to physical education and pursuit of marriage.

Still, Sammie's family represented to me everything that my own family wasn't. They trusted that kids could and would take care of themselves. I didn't like the abandonment, but I did envy the freedom and spontaneity.

My first years out of college I lived in several apartments by myself. When I'd think back on Sammie's family, I'd attempt to be more spontaneous about my own routine. I'd try to skip breakfast, to eat dinner while standing in my kitchen, to throw back my head the way Sammie did and bat my eyes at the cat.

It never worked. Within ten minutes I was back in my chair at the side of my new butcher-block table and the cat would be on his at the head. I'd be slowly chewing bread, drinking coffee, and staring out the window with the cat, or reading a book.

Now I'm married. At breakfast I sit at the same table, but now I stare at fifteen years' worth of scratches, rubbed to a homey old glow by daily wiping. I eat brown cereal and skim milk out of the chipped blue bowls that have been in my family since my grandmother pulled them out of detergent boxes in the Depression. My husband and two young children join me in weak morning conversation. At lunch the kids and I sit there to eat macaroni or peanut butter sandwiches. At dinnertime, we're all back again to eat something boring like fish sticks and rice, although for that meal we do attempt a little class by putting music on the stereo. The kids ignore it. They fight over the Mickey Mouse glasses. They pick the lentils out of their rice. They tell my husband about the bloody buffalo model they saw at the museum today.

It still amazes me that what we're doing around here is the preferred model of domestic life, that I can now come out of the closet about the routine of my life.

A lifetime's experience convinces me that what counts about eating at home is not so much the food as the routine. These patterns are not about imagination or creativity. That's why they're called routines.

Breakfast, lunch, and dinner are meals, not glamour concepts. It's okay, probably even good, if breakfast is always the same thing. That way the pre-schooler can pour Cheerios and the first adult in the kitchen can pop the toast into the toaster. No one needs more than a dish, a spoon, a glass for juice, and a napkin. Everybody knows this routine as well as Fred and Ginger knew how to waltz. That's okay. No one confuses simplicity with abandonment, because we are always there. Grace comes from doing well what we've done so many times before.

The evening meal is nearly the same in its simplicity. I don't entice family members with spectacular, personally tailored meals. We make one of the dozen or so meals my husband and I know how to prepare quickly, while whining children set the table. One of us yells, "Come and eat. Now!" We always, always turn off the TV. Music and candlelight are options— but not if the three-year-old is a pyromaniac, as ours is.

My husband and I try to converse pleasantly. Some day we hope the children will join us. Sometimes we recall our child-hoods. We ask the kids what they dreamed last night. We make it up as we go along.

As for creativity, I don't need to set the table in fancy ways or cut the children's breakfast toast into cookie-cutter shapes. Rituals are not about artifice but about acceptance. It is not our responsibility to embellish the world with cute decorations, but to make a place for the children in it. Maybe it is our adult responsibility to create the routines that will hold us together when the world cracks around us.

My sister died of cancer last summer. Through much of her final year she was racked with pain, nausea, and fatigue. Every morning she slept late to hoard her fleeting strength. Finally she got up, showered, and put on fresh clothes, in order to be sitting in the living room when her two children returned from school. For dinner she heated up one of the casseroles people brought in. Everyone sat in the right place at the table, ate the food, talked about what the kids had done at school, what her husband had done at work, what Karen had seen on her way to and from the doctor or the hospital—whatever.

That is ritual. That is saying that we are a family no matter what, and we will sit down together, and we will eat this food, and we will look at each other, and we will love each other in the fragility of an ordinary dinner. Within a week of Karen's death, her husband and children were back in their own places for meals. It may not be triumph, but it is survival.

That is the spirit in which I offer this reflection. Make room in your life for the continuity of family rituals. Sit together, eat together. Pay attention to your beloved children, to the grain of the wooden table, to the taste of the peach. Let it rest sweetly in your soul.

Divorced Father

LAURIE ABRAHAM

I have seen tears in my father's eyes twice: during the premiere of the Waltons' Christmas special and on the drive to his new apartment. If I had asked about the tears in his eyes the morning he left home, he probably would have blamed them on the sun. It was a too-bright day in June when my father left home, exactly eighteen years after my parents were married. He took his clothes, the old black-and-white TV, the popcorn popper, a pot and skillet, and a few other things. It took only two trips in the brown Pinto station wagon to move half of my father's life. Not that he couldn't have claimed his share of the tables, chairs, and pictures—but he chose to leave the fallout of two decades of acquiring with my mother.

From a house full of things, he went to an apartment of four empty rooms carpeted in gold-and-white shag. Soon, though, a queen-sized bed jutted from the middle of his bedroom wall, a butcher-block table with four matching chairs sat in the dining room, and an L-shaped brown velvet sofa dwarfed the 19-inch TV. He never bought a picture, a coffee-table, a knickknack or anything that said, "Harold Abraham lives here." A few things that my dad had claimed from the divorce, however, definitely bore his mark: cocktail glasses printed with the Dow Jones Industrial Average; four plastic beer mugs (one with the Bud Man, another with "Michelob" tastefully printed in gold); a stoneware coffee mug with sailboats. But these weren't the possessions of a father of two with a master's degree and a CPA degree. These were pieces of "Abe," that hard-drinking wild boy who wore garlic around his neck for a week to gain admission to a fraternity that stole a cow for a pet, a fraternity that was banned from the campus the year after my father left.

Money certainly didn't prevent my father from decorating his apartment. He usually had enough of it, and when he didn't, he spent it anyway. Surprisingly, the explanation for the starkness of his home came to me from people who have less in common with my father than my mother did: low-income teenagers who picked up trash and trimmed grass in a government jobs program.

"Where do you stay?" several of them asked me during the summer that I worked as their supervisor. At first I wondered about their word choice: I always asked new acquaintances where they lived, not where they stayed. But after listening to them all summer I understood why "stay" was the most appropriate word to describe their experiences. They were always moving, from their mother's apartment, to their grandmother's, to an aunt's. None of these places were necessarily bad, just temporary. These kids didn't live at East Seventy-fifth and Superior, they stayed there for a time. My father was doing that, too—staying. He had no intention of living in his apartment, or calling it home. It was a way station between his first wife and the one to come—except on Sundays. When his girls came to visit, my dad rushed to throw together a home.

I know little about my father's childhood, but I won't forget the few memories that he's let slip over the years. He slept in a dresser drawer because his family could not afford a crib. His dad never said to him, "Harold, how was school today?" He went without many of the furnishings that make up a home, never mind the nurturing. Making a home for his children was important so that he could give us what he never got. He did his best—for us and for the boy whose parents never quite made it to his high school football games.

But since he had been deprived of the emotional sustenance that makes a home a home, my father was never quite sure what to do with my sister and me once he had us. He relied on food—the most straightforward kind of nurturing—to turn his bachelor's apartment into a home. Breakfast was pancakes. In the beginning, when all three of us were trying to fight off sadness and before my sister and I grew to resent the Sunday morning call, "Your father's here," he flipped them. By high school, the pancakes didn't fly and I slumped in my chair, suffering from the six-pack I had downed the night before. By dinner I'd usually recovered enough to enjoy either spaghetti with Ragú sauce or Kentucky Fried Chicken—always carry-out; the restaurant wasn't home. These dishes were hearty but deliciously junky, the kind of food men with few cooking skills and one chance a week to win their children's approval are apt to serve. Between meals, we'd eat some more: popcorn or pizza rolls while watching football on TV, or ice cream after an awkward, time-filling walk in the woods.

My father's homemaking hit full stride at Christmas, when the shortcomings we never could ignore became that much more obvious and sad. First, we'd pick the right tree with my mother. Then, another tree with Dad, if we could arrange a time that was "mutually convenient." To the scratchy strains of "Christmas in Killarney," a Ray Coniff album my parents bought when they were first married, we pushed the lights onto the prickly branches of a spruce or Scotch pine. (We never used garden gloves with my father, although my mother used them; he probably didn't own a pair anyway.) My father's half of the ornaments included a few of the "good" ones—the papier-mâché Santa, the Ohio State football helmet trimmed with holly—but he also had his share of the back-of-the-tree duds such as clear plastic teardrops, one for each of the twelve days of Christmas. Most years, decorating the tree with Dad was fun, but to my sister and me, it wasn't our *real* tree in our *real* home. It was what we put up with Dad so he wouldn't be lonely at Christmas.

Long after I began to consider the two times I saw my father almost cry, I realized that there might be a connection between the tears of moving day and those provoked by the Waltons' Christmas show. Its plot was this: Pa Walton was lost during a snowstorm on Christmas Eve. A man was cut off from his family. I doubt back then, watching that show, that Dad imagined one day he would be driving away from his wife and girls, but somehow he identified. And what my father missed the most when he left home was something the Waltons had plenty of—people. That's what my father was forced to give up: lots of people around, people he might not necessarily be close to (like my mom), but who were present. He didn't want to struggle to build a new family from scratch; he needed to be plopped down in the middle of one. And so he was, finally. His second wife comes from a large and raucous family, and my dad has three new stepchildren. Large Christmas Eve parties at his new wife's home have become something of a tradition for us.

For me, the parties are events. I wear red, or something that stands out in a crowd of relatives I see once a year. Yet although I always have a good time, I still feel that my real Christmas is the next day at treeside, in those more intense, heartfelt moments with my mother. Spending the day with my mother is what I want, but I do not think I could enjoy myself if my father were alone on Christmas. He would never ask my sister or me to spend part of the day with him; he is too proud. Instead, he would call us around eleven in the morning to wish us "Merry Christmas" in a loud voice. His conversation would be punctuated by laughs that seemed to end before they started. I knew from experience that when he wasn't talking, he was gritting his teeth slightly, tightening the line of his jaw. "Love you big bunches," he would say rapidly, before hanging up. Then the phone would ring again right away. He had forgotten to tell me that I left my sweatshirt at his apartment. "Oh, thanks, Dad; I'll get it next time we come over," I would say.

"Okay, then. Merry Christmas."

"Merry Christmas, Dad."

I am grateful to my new stepfamily for sheltering my father and me from this coldest cold. Without them, my father would get lost in the snow.

Socks

LAURA GREEN

As a metaphor for domestic life, the sock is hard to beat. In pairs, it represents the allure of domesticity; alone, it is a reproachful reminder of domestic frustrations. Socks in pairs are the Platonic ideal, the perfection and orderliness that households rarely achieve—and then only for a flicker of time. The single sock, like a lot of people pulled into domesticity, secretly prefers the solo life and pairs off only when forced.

Either way, the sock epitomizes some of the finer things—the goals, if you will—of domestic life. A sock is a well-designed object, with the same functional elegance as a kitchen match or a three-legged stool. It warms your feet, covers your homely shins, and keeps your shoes from causing blisters. There is no waste in a sock, no difficulty using it. It has passed the test of time. It goes beyond function to comfort, the not-insignificant difference that separates a privy from a bathroom.

Like a welcoming room, a sock reflects the owner's personality. I myself would not wear white anklets with purple palm trees on them, though my daughter used to. I doubt if she would go for my solid black silk models, though I wear them with slacks all the time. Even though sock stores are not what they used to be, the sock still is a peek-a-boo opportunity for personal expression. Yellow argyles, op-art checks, jacquard patterns, pulsing neon stripes, Snoopys on parade, Christmas trees with sequin ornaments, and my favorites, thick slouch socks, hang alongside those characterless mutts, the one-size-fits-all tube socks.

The sock stands for ease and well-being, goals of any sane domestic policy; imagine what would happen in the average office if the staff felt free enough to walk around in their socks. Unfortunately, you can't take your shoes off at the office; you can only do it at home. Feeling at home and walking around in your socks are practically the same things. To paraphrase Robert Frost, home is the place where they have to let you walk around in your socks, because in all likelihood they are shoeless themselves.

Socks, particularly single socks, also embody everything that is maddening, boring, and useless about domesticity. Socks create the worst, dreariest sort of make-work. From the day you bring them home from the store, socks require care out of all proportion to the services they provide in return. Socks need to be put away, found, worn, washed, dried, folded or balled up, put away, worn, thrown in a corner, found, washed and dried—an endless cycle of obligation and loss. Sooner or later, one sock takes off and the other hangs around, as reproachful as a child on a rainy Sunday. Three or four people changing their socks every day guarantee that a woman always has some busywork to do.

You can get metaphysical about socks if you like, pondering the grace of their design, their stubborn, catlike refusal to be team players, their bachelor-like tendencies to pair off unpredictably, and so on, but I think that may be like looking for the cosmos in a pebble: you can do it, but it takes a high level of belief.

Just as socks symbolize that most known of worlds, the house, I suspect they also mark the end of the known world. They may be the last familiar object between man and the depths of the universe. I am convinced that when the first space vehicle reaches the edge of the void, the cameras will send back pictures of an eerie but familiar zone. Out of the great nothing will float blue and red and striped and torn socks, each single, each drifting weightlessly, endlessly, dreamlike. Man will finally be in the place where lost socks have been all along. In limbo.

Playing House

MARY BETH DANIELSON

It is summer. If I looked down and saw little-girl shorts, a plain white T-shirt, and Band-aids on my legs, I wouldn't be surprised. I'd know just what to do: Go find Kathy Miller, go with her to the back of her yard where the pine woods start, and play house.

Those were the summers. Inside four roped-off pine trees, we created an all-encompassing world of beauty and drama. We arranged furniture—old shelves and end tables from her parent's garage, Christmas-present doll furniture, mysterious structures fashioned from rocks and cement blocks and scrap lumber. We decorated with wildflowers from the woods and garden flowers arranged in tin cans. We set the table with doll dishes, platters of leaves, and bowls of pine cones. Day after day, by the edge of that deep, buzzing woods, we invented a wonderful domestic life.

I still love to play house. I like homemaking when it demands my imagination and resourcefulness. As a child I stood in the playhouse, arms folded, wondering what we needed, and then imagining what in the world I could use as a substitute. I do exactly the same thing now. Then pine cones would usually do; now it's more complicated, but the same part of my imagination is at work. Domestic life at its richest seems to be a series of needs to which we respond with creative and ingenious solutions, with a natural and organic creativity.

It's a quarter to nine in the morning and the kids are already bored and fussy. I can yell at them, try to ignore them, or think of a solution. This time I choose to think. With some effort I get them both dressed and out the door, so that ten minutes later what you see is a serious toddler in a blue cap watering the flowers all by herself, and a baby flopping up and down on a quilt spread on the lawn.

I'm twenty-two, it's my first year in the city, and I'm always broke, but I want a Christmas tree. I buy a two-dollar tree from the tree merchant's scrap pile, take it home, and lean it in the corner of my living room. I decorate it with three bona fide ornaments and forty spray-shellacked pretzel twists. It looks happy, and I leave it there until Groundhog's Day.

One day I clean, dust, and clear away the ordinary stacks of papers, magazines, and books that clutter the dining table. Suddenly, the room looks bare. I stand there with my arms across my chest and think. Of course. A centerpiece. A basket of pine cones.

At its best domestic life is satisfying. We solve problems, find beauty, keep things rolling along. Home becomes a sanctuary for our imaginations, a place where the little girl in us still plays.

But not always. One year my parents gave me a dollhouse for Christmas. When I first opened the box, I was ecstatic. It was made of printed metal. Outside it looked like a small suburban ranch home. Inside it had three rooms—kitchen, living room, and bedroom. It came with turquoise and coral molded plastic furniture. I played with it for a while, but there simply was not much one could do to it. How interesting is a kitchen with curtains printed right on the wall at the die-cut windows? The refrigerator and stove were press-stamped plastic boxes that didn't even open. When I tried to jazz up the interior, my pine cone solutions looked homely. After a few days I abandoned the dollhouse and went back to shoeboxes furnished with fabric scraps and folded paper.

Sometimes I still feel as if I'm playing house with that storebought tin model. I move the pieces around but nothing comforts or feels like true home. It's as if I am arranging someone else's dreams. I feel cramped and stifled. If it goes on too long, I well up with anger.

Solutions for this alienation vary, but I know they have worked when my house turns back into my home. Then it is neither a prison nor a hideout, but a place to think and create and experiment with the important and the trivial. It is my makeshift dollhouse in the woods.

Getting and Keeping

NANCY EBERLE

We tend to think of housework in terms o washing, wiping, putting away—in other words, a series of discrete, repetitive tasks. Wrong. What housework is mostly about is Getting and Keeping.

Getting dog food for the month. Getting Perrier and brie for the evening. Getting Sarah to her violin lesson. Getting Sarah's hand-me-downs to cousin Susie. Getting the medical bills together for the insurance company. Getting the car to the garage, getting the books back to the library, getting the sitter home.

And then there's Keeping. Keeping on top of Sarah's violin practice. Keeping the dog in dog food. Keeping the medical bills in a file. Keeping in mind that the library books are due on Wednesday, the sitter can't sit on Thursdays, the garage is taking Fridays off in February, and you're out of Perrier.

Getting is basically physical, performed on foot and in cars. Keeping is done in the head and is responsible for many of our headaches. In any breakdown of housework by gender, it will quickly be apparent that although both sexes may Get, it is largely women who Keep. There are exceptions, of course. Men willingly, even gladly, undertake such keeping tasks as worrying about whether a new roof will be needed in 1995, or a paint job before the summer of '92. But even in the area of maintenance, it can be argued that most of the keeping work is done in the heads of women. Shopping provides a perfect example of the politics of Getting and Keeping. Men are wont to assert "Women shop; men buy," as if the former were some sort of child's play and only the act of a plastic credit card snapping down on a glass counter meant anything. Whereas in truth, shopping is to family life as curating is to museums, acquisitioning is to a library, and matériel is to armies.

There are certain lessons to be drawn from all this. One is that in a house where the Getting is done mainly by one person and the Keeping by another, a superior/inferior relationship will prevail. Just as a general outranks a private and a film director outranks a cameraman, a Keeper outranks a Getter.

Therefore, in a house where equality is the goal, Keeping as well as Getting should be shared—unless, of course, the woman prefers to be the general or director (or Director General), which in many cases she does. The problem with this choice is the lack of respect that accrues to the Keeping tasks. For the issue here is not who Gets and who Keeps but giving Keeping its due. People don't quit jobs, by and large, because they have to work too hard, but because of inadequate recognition of just how hard they have to work.

Few of us have houseKeepers, but all of us have houses to Keep. Let us demand for the job the respect it deserves. Resolve to be amused no longer by snide references to time spent shopping. Cut off at the pass all comments about persnicketiness. Do not apologize for planning ahead. In short, decline to be demeaned. Any job well done deserves respect.

Friday Night Dinner

CARROLL STONER

I used to entertain: real dinner parties, with planned guest lists and menus culled from cookbooks. I called or sent invitations weeks in advance to invite friends and occasionally people we'd met and liked and wanted to know better. I think it made me feel grown-up.

Then one year a while back I stopped having dinner parties. Just like that. Something didn't feel right about those well-planned, thoroughly organized, nothing-impromptu-about-this-gathering occasions. They weren't exactly boring, but there was something juiceless about them. Or maybe dinner parties were just part of a stage that I had passed through.

As a substitute, I started having people in for dinner, which might sound like the same thing but isn't. I invite friends in on

Friday evenings, tell them to come right from work, and explain that it is not a dinner party but rather an extended-family gathering. Soon after I started this, two out of every four Fridays were "parties," and more than one set of friends told me they looked forward to being invited.

Preparations for my Friday Night Family Dinners are entirely different from dinner party plans, mainly because they are so low-key. I usually plan my grocery shopping for the day before and buy whatever looks good, is specially priced, and inspires me to want to cook. I might set the table before leaving for my office that morning. Otherwise, it's a family dinner with a few extra touches.

The food is different from "dinner-party food." I have, for example, become expert at dishes that take more arranging than cooking. (Empty a jar of roasted red Italian-style peppers onto a plate of curly-leafed lettuce. Drape a few anchovies on top, put a small pile of good black olives on one end of the plate, drizzle with olive oil—or don't bother—serve with Italian bread, and you have an instant hors d'oeuvre.) I frequently put friends and family to work, or just give them a glass of wine in the kitchen so they can keep me company. Sometimes we have such a good time in the kitchen that it's almost anticlimactic to sit down and eat.

I could tell you what I serve (pasta or sautéed things, or oven-roasted meats or cook-ahead stews, or even, in extremis, order-in pizza), but that would be beside the main point, which is that my new mode of "entertaining" has done wonders for my family and my social life. Whether friends are invited or not, attendance is mandatory for our children, including the college-age son who has moved into his first apartment. The meal is served somewhat like Sunday dinner used to be when I grew up—we use good dishes and linens, light candles, set the table with silver and wineglasses, and make a family ritual out of it.

Often, we'll have hors d'oeuvres in the living room, but just as frequently we snack on something in the kitchen while we're getting the meal on the table. Everyone helps. The two children have their responsibilities and no longer even complain about having to set the table or clear the dishes, pour water into water glasses, or dig out linen napkins. They don't complain because it's become an old, familiar routine, and routines are good for families.

Just as important, these somewhat informal gatherings have helped us define what we want in our friendships. We have discovered, for example, that the kind of people we want as friends have to feel comfortable in a family setting. I'm not talking crying babies or teenagers who never stop talking, by the way, although either could happen and not totally disrupt things; home life, after all, is not a carefully staged opera production. I'm talking about a kind of warmth, an atmosphere in which people can feel comfortable bringing children or coming alone, and in which the children, including grown ones, can stick around for the conversation, if it interests them—or wander away from the table when they get bored with talk of politics or business or gossip or us.

Young people, I hope, learn subtle lessons (and some not so subtle) in this environment. When we adults are in a talkative mood, they learn to compete for time in the spotlight. They are encouraged to articulate their beliefs, emboldened by others' approval or sometimes stopped in their tracks by disagreement. When it works, they are nourished in far more substantial ways than by food. I hope it helps them mature, and I see small, hopeful signs that this is so. My college-age son has never gotten over the accidental revelation by a friend that one of our mutual friends, now in her forties, still likes to smoke dope. Is that good or bad? I put it in the category of real life.

The choice of Friday evening did not start out tied to my husband's religious roots, where Saturday is Sabbath, starting when the candles are lit at sundown on Friday. This ceremony commemorates the weekly family holiday that is celebrated, as most Jewish holidays are, around the dinner table. Friday nights were my choice, because they start the weekend with a bang and are a dividing line between work and family life. Although these nights don't initiate the weekly day of rest that the Ten Commandments tell us to use for reflection, we do use weekends for revitalization. And Friday night dinners get them off to a good start.

DRAWING
THE LINE

Dogs

JANICE ROSENBERG

If your child can make crumbs with a banana and you're not always a foot away with a sponge to wipe up his messes, consider buying a dog. Dogs are fun to have around the house. They fetch balls and make you laugh when they chase their tails. They're always ready to go for a walk or listen to your problems. They're never judgmental, and when you have a few spare minutes they're nice to pet.

All that's obvious, but the best (and least celebrated) thing a dog can do is help out in the kitchen. A small dog built low to the ground, preferably one with a good nose, is best for this job. Dogs will spend hours lying in wait under kitchen tables during kiddie feedings. No scrap or blob is too meager or too revolting.

Careful training can raise a dog's natural crumbing instincts to elegant heights. A simple, low whistle followed by a tap of the foot in the right direction can rouse a snoozing dog to attend to almost any spill. Sensitive hearing makes this a simple matter. A Chicago doctor tells me that since she took to giving her dachshund leftover egg yolks, he wakes at any noise that resembles the creaky opening of a styrofoam egg carton. The sound of the refrigerator door is the call of the wild for many a housebound canine. Dog owners quickly learn to avoid long reflective moments in the cool refrigerated air, since dogs can scarf down mass quantities of comestibles from lower shelves in the time it takes humans to decide between Coke and Canada Dry.

Dogs need not confine their kitchen talents to the obvious. All dog owners will tell you that after they've fried a passel of chicken, any dog worth its salt will tongue-clean the linoleum around the frying area to an immaculate spit shine. Dogs seek refreshment in odd places. They retrieve year-old potato chips from underneath refrigerators, free desiccated Spaghetti O's from high-chair seats and sift through mounds of paper trash for the single prechewed wad of bubble gum. They launch sneak attacks during the unloading of grocery bags and boxes. A teacher I know in Salem, Oregon, found her Airedale puppy under the living room coffee table polishing off a half-pound bag of bulgur that she had just brought home from the store. For several days afterward, his thievery caused the disruption of both his digestion and his owner's sleep.

Guilt over discarded leftovers is a dead issue once you have a dog. In this case, the bigger the animal the better you'll feel. Dogs love scraps and can keep you from eating them yourself. They do not discriminate according to national cuisine or excellence of preparation. Raw is as good as well done. With everlasting endurance, they sit dumbly drooling as their owners skin chicken breasts or separate strips of bacon. But meat is not all to a dog. Anything soaked in oil, from a cucumber slice to a paper towel, will do. For this reason you must find a trash can with a lid that would defeat an engineer. A car mechanic once told me he felt certain that his step-to-open kitchen garbage can would foil his two-year-old boxer, but the dog mastered its secret in no time. Desperate, the man set a mousetrap on the closed lid. Although the dog incurred no physical harm, the snap apparently gave her quite a fright. Soon, just the mere sight of the unset trap was enough to keep her away from even the most aromatic refuse. The trick is to teach them what's allowed within their territory and what's off limits.

Dogs love to graze in open dishwashers, licking spaghetti sauce from dinner plates and cake batter from mixing spoons. A collie who specialized in dishwasher patrol learned to distinguish clean dishes from dirty. She never came around, not even to sniff, during the regular morning unloadings. (Note well, however, that care must be taken to prevent removal of unwashed items to the living room couch.)

Friends in Cincinnati own a dog of mixed ancestry who does frying pan clean-ups. He specializes in burned-on scrambled egg scraps, but in fact will tackle burned-on anything. Placing one paw in the pan, he uses his bottom front teeth to scrape it completely clean. Although Teflon surfaces do not take well to this method, nothing works better on cast iron.

City folklore includes the story of a woman who used the family bulldog to drive away a pair of guests who repeatedly dropped in, uninvited, at dinnertime. One night after feeding these moochers for the third time, she set all the dinner plates on the floor and let the dog lick them clean. To the guests' horror, she placed the dishes back in the cabinet when they were spotless. The guests were never seen again.

A visitor once asked a friend why the dog sat next to her during dinner. Because you're sitting in his place, she was told. Whether or not the guest has usurped a dog's place at table, he will always sit near any newcomers to check out their slob quotient. Dogs quickly learn who offers the best odds. A springer spaniel I know always greets Grandpa effusively and sits beside him waiting for dessert. Grandpa, a frequent visitor, is the only person who's ever fed him cherry pie.

Nothing beats a dog for company in the kitchen. Dogs never criticize the cooking. They don't care if you nibble before meals; a musician friend says that unlike her family and friends, her beagle never scolds her for between-meal snacking. And a dog never tattles when you take a taste and then stick the spoon in the pot without washing it.

In sum, dogs do far more around the house than offer

protection from burglars. Their abilities as housekeepers in the kitchen deserve recognition. While a mini-vac can handle crumbs, how many times has one rested its muzzle on any-one's lap and looked up with big, wet soulful brown eyes waiting for the steak bone that is payment for a job well done?

Television

LAURA GREEN

Our third or fourth television ban is going on now. They come and go according to some rhythm that must be more obvious to others than it is to us. While they work, I am a happy woman, even though I have to give up television news, (which I enjoy not only for its news value but because I'm an old print reporter and like to make fun of what I see on the local news).

Let me make my position on television clear. I like it when I like it, when I'm a certain kind of depressed, or when it's New Year's Day. But for the most part, I want it out of my life, and I'm stubborn enough to get my way.

The cycle goes something like this. I am working long hours and want to spend time with my family when I come home. The kids' grades are starting to slide. My son's friendships are playing second fiddle to reruns. I raise hell and things are so bad that my husband agrees to haul three or four televisions (he'd found a justification for buying each one) down into the basement, and I call the cable company and cancel.

After the initial sulk, which lasts three or four days, it's not as bad as you might think. The kids complain that they are

becoming social retards because they don't know what everyone is talking about. Still, they manage. They get more homework done. Jenny begins reading books, a crazy salad of pop
novels one week, Mark Twain the next, and Mario Vargas
Llosa the week after that. Nick gets out his baseball cards—
not a bad hobby for a boy who wants to be Don Mattingly
when he grows up. They play with their friends more often. I
am happy.

Then, complacency sets in. A set comes up on weekends,
and, one Sunday night, it doesn't go back down; the set is a
big one, and the basement steps are steep. My husband complains, with some justification, about the hauling. Then comes
a vacation. Faced with being meaner than I can justify and
confronting the possibility of having to play Monopoly for
three weeks straight, I knuckle under and let the big set stay
up. We have an orgy of videotaping. Vacation ends and the set
stays. The kids go through the motions of homework in front
of the set. Someone gets a D. My husband slips into a coma
while watching.

About this time, the Los Angeles effect reaches our dinner
table. Good dinner table conversation at our house is difficult
to begin with because our schedules guarantee that all five of
us will be at the table no more than four nights a week. But
television changes the way children talk. Discourse, such as it
is, disappears, and chatter takes its place. I, who am hungry for
discussion, get a meager slice of empty sitcom calories. My
son's sense of humor changes from screwy, endearing little
boy jokes to one-liners. Untampered with, Nick's humor runs
on, a zany, verbal *Bolero* of shaggy-dog stories. When the
televisions are around, instead of telling weird tales from the
fifth grade, he sits at the table flipping bits of hamburger to
the dog, saying things like "Live it up, baby, this is Holly-
wood!" He parrots Los Angeles one-liners, the stuff comedy
writers grind out on the balconies of their condominiums.

About then I lose it and the sets go back down to the
basement and we start again.

There is simply no way to win the television argument when you take the con side. As the bearer of bad news, you play the nerdy part; but in this play the senior class will never rally to your side before the drama is over. Though hardly anyone disputes that you get more and better things done when there's no tube around, they like you better if you go somewhere and don't watch instead of trying to uplift them. I know this, but like someone who ups and joins a temperance club instead of just refusing to drink, I can't help myself.

Television does violence to all my notions that I live a life of at least some good taste. In my last corner of self-delusion, the place where the novel gets written, the books get read, the bon mots are created, in that never-never land where my stomach is flat and my mind is sharp, there is no television. Television is somewhere over *there* in the same place as the hair rollers, macaroni dinners, and bridge night.

I've made my point. Yes, the quality of verbal life did improve; yes, the grades went up; yes, I was right and they knew it. Trouble is, I miss the set too. I like to watch a little TV. I want to do it on my terms. I like to curl up under a lap throw and watch old movies from time to time. I miss renting movies from the video store. I miss the news.

When I'm feeling this way, my husband reminds me that the desire to keep the television in the closet means we presume we are capable of replacing it with something better, not just something else. He's got me there. I can no more guarantee an interesting evening than can the television. We're not exactly Edith, Archie, and Meathead, but when we're left to discuss the topics closest to our hearts, I complain about money, Jenny complains about boys, Nick complains about minor aches and pains, my stepson Noah reminisces about his other life in California, and my husband doesn't talk at all. Familiarity with our conversations can breed contempt. I'm happy for the most part, but I have to admit that, conversationally, we work on the same principle as computers. You can stop putting televised garbage in but you can still get garbage out.

Saying No

MARY BETH DANIELSON

I am a woman, which means I was reared to say yes in all situations (except for one—but that is another essay). The reasons for this constant yea-saying are much publicized. However, just because a thing is talked about a lot doesn't mean anyone is doing anything about it. So I propose something really radical. I propose we revive an old strategy, used by countless women from Lysistrata on down. I propose we quit. No recriminations, no guilt, just put a stop to the endless catering we do.

Imagine. Ten minutes before supper is served, my two-and-a-half-year-old looks up at me and lisps, "I wanna paint, Mommy." I say no. She is crestfallen, she cries, and I let her cry. She won't turn into a stifled, unexpressed, inexpressive toddler. I assume that feeding the baby, making supper, and setting the table really is enough for me and I suggest she go watch TV. Expressing her feelings through art is fine, but I also want her to know that grown women say no.

Imagine. Christmas is coming soon. Your mother, mother-in-law, grandmother, and brother's family all expect you to visit on Christmas Day. It sounds awful. You do not have a magic sleigh or reindeer that fly through the air. You just have a car that slogs through holiday traffic like all the rest. You also have human children in your family, and they get cranky after seventy minutes of company manners in houses with no toys. And when you stop to think about it, so do you. After years of making the rounds, you say no. You stay home and invite over the people you like the best. You let the kids wear whatever they want and you don't investigate when you hear small crashes upstairs. You just drink another eggnog and chat with the adults. You learn secondhand that you have so offended some relatives that they are not going to even invite you next year. You can live with that.

Imagine. Your husband wants to make love. You don't. You say no. Neither of you says anything for a while. Then you tell him you have never faked it (well, hardly ever, and there's no need to offend him now) and you don't want to start. Lovemaking drops off like a rock sinking to the bottom of a murky lake. But you decide you're tired of rote sex. Your husband brings you flowers. You actually go out on a date. You see a romantic movie on your trusty VCR. And then, one evening you make love again and it is wonderful. You said no, but with patience what you got back was a better yes.

Saying no, like most of the important things in life, is risky business. It means you are about to discover just how much people love you, instead of how much they take for granted the services you provide. It means you are looking at yourself in a new way, and that you are asking others to do the same. It means you are respecting yourself full-time, not just in the odd scraps of time that no one else wants.

Saying no means you are going to discover some wonderful things, like the fact that no one in your family misses six-layer cakes or ironed pillowcases. That there is no reason to feel grateful for a job that underpays and overexpects. That others rarely value a person more than she values herself. You can't learn to say no overnight, but as any woman who has struggled over the years to learn self-respect will tell you, it is well worth the wait.

Children, Other People's

JANICE ROSENBERG

For ten years, we three couples and our six kids have held an annual Hanukkah party. The party rotated from house to house and I always dreaded my turn. This year, as I set platters of potato pancakes on the buffet, I realize I'm actually enjoying myself. I'm not muttering to myself about how rotten the kids are. Of course I didn't mean *my* boys. The *other* kids made me furious.

There was a time when, just because I like my adult friends, it didn't follow that I liked their children. Ellis and Jackie came to our house often when their girls were small. The older one took the cushions off the nubby beige couch and spread them around the living room. Then, with her shoes on, she leapt from one to the next, pretending live alligators patrolled the canals in between.

"What an imagination," Ellis said.

Their younger daughter walked on windowsills. Whether the third-floor windows were open or closed, she did her acrobatic routine.

"Great balance," Jackie said. "I think I'll sign her up for ballet when she's out of diapers."

And then there were the twins, Sam and Tony. While we ate dinner, Sam scaled the ladder on the back of my dining room chair to sit triumphantly on my shoulders. His brother emptied floor to ceiling bookshelves. He then built book towers and knocked them down.

"They're so easily entertained," their father said. "We never have to drag toys along."

At least their parents were consistent. Once I found Tony in his own kitchen standing on the counter wearing muddy boots and eating chocolate chips out of a cereal bowl with a spoon. "Tony, darling," his mother said, "why don't you share those with your friends?"

And my kids? Sure, they were mischievous. My older son liked to play a game that he called Pie. He based it on a "Sesame Street" routine in which a chef, precariously carrying several pies, shouted out their number and then tripped and dropped them in a heap. In any other child's room, my son would pull all the toys and games down from the shelves, dump boxes of Legos, Lincoln Logs, and jigsaw puzzles on the floor, and then yell "Pie!" and roll around in the debris. When we visited friends, I sometimes forgot about Pie until I heard the crash. But upon finding the mess, did I say, "How creative! How wonderfully yet harmlessly expressive of his anal aggressive urges"? No, I sighed, apologized, and made him help clean up.

My younger son had subtler skills. He liked fixing things with a toy screwdriver that he carried in the pocket of his overalls. Whenever we went visiting I made sure he parked it at the door. At least that's what I did after the business with the fifteen kitchen cabinet handles. When he took them off and put them back on upside down, did I say, "Imagine such sustained effort and coordination in a three-year-old! And such vision! He's not at all inhibited by spatial conventions"? No, I told him that we couldn't go home until he turned the handles right side up.

For years I dreaded visits from free-spirited children who poked through my dresser drawers and ate pâté out of my refrigerator with their hands. I gritted my teeth and lifted the kids off my couch cushions as gently as I could; I suggested

that they sit *at* the table instead of on it, and I hoped the
weather would be fine so that all of us could go out to the
park. I moved kids with Play-Doh from my Oriental rug to
the kitchen table. Grape juice never darkened my door and
finger-painting sessions took place on the back porch.

But my efforts made no impression on my friends. I knew
that they considered me uptight, compulsive, a spoilsport, and
a crank. I considered them ill-mannered and inconsiderate,
dupes of children for whom they set no limits.

It's a wonder, I think, as I look around the room at this
Hanukkah party, that we managed to stay friends. But a
bigger wonder is what happened to those awful kids. I watch
Jackie's older daughter daintily dab a bit of sour cream from
her chin. One of my sons requests the applesauce, and a
twin—is it Tony or Sam?—passes it smoothly down the table.
Is it possible that my style of raising kids is not the only one
that works?

As our kids devour desert, the grown-up conversation turns
to problems we as parents are just beginning to encounter:
dating, driving, drinking, drugs. Facing these problems, I do
not feel that old confidence—or do I mean dogmatism?—about
how they should be handled. To be honest, I could use some
help. Ten years ago I could not imagine consulting these
friends. But tonight, seeing that their methods worked as well
as mine to bring infants to this reasonable stage, I think that I
will listen to what each has to say.

$\mathcal{H}$ousework

LAURA GREEN

Consider the pot of soup on the stove. Big chunks of carrots, hastily scraped and chopped, hunks of chicken, onion, celery, orzo, grease. No subtlety at all. I, who used to be something of a cook, now make simple soup for fast meals that pay lip service to healthy eating. Their real purpose is to get us to the table by seven thirty.

I used to cook elaborate, time-consuming dishes. I used to spend weeks sewing slipcovers. It was easy. I lived by myself and had plenty of spare time. Cleaning for one doesn't take long, particularly when you remember how difficult it is for one person to really dirty up a place and how easy it is to be tolerant of your own mess. Homemaking under those circumstances is not much harder than playing house.

Then one day I went to the emergency room to have a cut sewn up and my life changed. I met a medical student with big blue eyes, long blond hair, and granny glasses. Before I could say, "Here's my phone number," we were living together and I had indignantly carted his ex-wife's electric knife out to the alley and he had stowed my ex-husband's Polish opera posters in the basement. In what seemed like days, I was washing dishes for two, then doing laundry for three, then picking up after four. Home was still a place where I could find deep satisfaction, but only when everything else was done. Instead of sitting back to marvel at what I had created at

186

the end of the day, I looked around and saw unfinished
chores, chores that multiplied like the walking brooms from
the *Sorcerer's Apprentice.*

Housekeeping was no longer a joy but a job and not nearly
as interesting as my other one at the newspaper. At work I
was a reporter, running all over the place. When I got home, I
wanted to stop running, not start up again. I attacked my
chores with great anger because they were *my* chores, not *our*
chores. It was one thing to mop the kitchen floor when you are
alone in your own place. It is quite another to do it while your
husband and children are lying on the couch watching the
World Series. You become as resentful as Cinderella while
everyone is off at the ball.

The unfortunate truth is that for too many women, home is
a place we make nice for other people. We leave ourselves out
of the equation. Before long, the pleasure we once took in the
house is buried under a pile of chores. It takes a clearheaded,
confident soul to remember that domesticity ought to be equated
with enjoyment first, shelter second, and picking up dead last.

Not that it is easy to swim upstream. I know only two wives
who said, "I'm not cleaning up after you." One was the wife of
a reporter. He walked into the city room at the office after his
weekend honeymoon and told us that the morning after the
wedding, he asked his wife to make him some coffee. She
counteroffered with a can of Coke. That way, she explained,
she wouldn't have to get out of bed. And when he was done,
he could toss the can in the garbage can and there would be
nothing to wash. The marriage lasted about four years, a good
three years longer than predicted. I do not know what role, if
any, Coca-Cola played in its demise.

The other wife who refused to pick up is my oldest friend.
She is selectively, creatively domestic and she has never confused domesticity with nitpicking. She cleans what she has to
clean and doesn't fuss over it. What she does is sew, although
to call it sewing is like calling Michelangelo's *David* a statue of
a naked man. It's more fair to say she uses a needle and thread

to make art. Over the years, she has come home from work to
sew wall hangings you could look at all day—bold visions of
hamburgers, of ant farms, of polar bears fishing through the
ice. She makes my children wonderful dolls with painted faces
and wild black dreadlocks. She sends them hand-sewn whales
with baby whales inside, and parrots of bright-flowered silk.
She knows her domestic priorities and she is not about to let a
pile of unfolded laundry come between her and her sewing
machine.

Maybe this approach only works well for those people, like
my friends who live alone, and maybe they live alone because
they take this approach to life. But even if you aren't as free
to redefine housework as they were, there is still something to
be said for going halfway. Home ought to be a place where
you feel free to browse through old photos when you need to
grocery shop, a place where you can sprawl on the bed with a
book and ignore the cobwebs on the walls. A domestic life
worthy of the name must have time built into it for things you
love well as chores. But more often than not, home is like that
Thurber drawing of the apprehensive man walking toward the
house that is turning into a looming scold. Women know that
Thurber could just as well have drawn a woman coming up
the walk as a man.

The reason I wrote this piece is that a bad back forced me to
do what my friend had been urging me to do for years—let go.
For one month last winter, I was confined to bed with a
slipped disc, allowed up for one shower a day and as many
bathroom trips as were unavoidable. I wish I could tell you
that I snuggled in and had a wonderful time, but I didn't—at
least not right away. For the first week, I was so miserable in
my impotence that I bellowed orders at anyone who was
foolish enough to walk by the bedroom door: "Take out the
trash!" "Change the dog's water" "Run the dishwasher right
this minute!" My children took routes through the house that
kept them from my line of sight. They put on headphones so
they couldn't hear me while I raged and wept like Lear on the

moor. It took me days to understand that my options were either taking it easy and getting better or driving myself crazy. Frankly, I think I did the right thing only because the alternative was back surgery.

Eventually I settled in. I worked the *New York Times* crossword puzzles—in ink, the mark of arrogance. I read books. I wrote with my computer keyboard on a pillow on my stomach and the terminal on a card table by the bed. My husband dragged the television and the VCR upstairs and I watched old movies, sometimes with a bed full of children and the dog in the middle. My students came over to visit. After a while, I stopped caring whether there were greasy dishes in the sink or wet clothes growing mildew in the drier—as I assumed there were. Because I had no choice but to stop bossing everyone and start having a good time, my slipped disc was the proverbial painful lesson.

I don't know why I can't let go, and I'm not sure I care to find out what makes me such a control freak. But I did learn this: Home has to sustain you. If not, it becomes a house of horrors. So it's simple soup for now. The four of us make a mass attack on the house on Sunday morning and we hold the cleaning to two hours. I try not to yell about the laundry, the garbage, the wet towels on the floor.

On my first trip down the stairs after I was allowed to walk again, I saw hundreds of dots on the wall, a great gray wave of fingerprints undulating its way down the stairway wall. Oh, well. Someday, someone, probably me, will clean it up. But I'm not going to worry about it right now. And even though something still goes clack in the small of my back whenever I roll over, I never felt better.

Kid's Room

JANICE ROSENBERG

When we moved to our new house, each of our sons had a room of his own for the first time ever. As soon as all the unpacking was done, both boys went into their rooms and shut their doors—on us and especially on each other. They'd suffered through twelve years of rooming together and that was more than enough.

The room they first shared held a single bed, a crib, and tons of toys. For years they did not question being together, believing what we said about the benefits of having company and the convenience of having all their toys in one place. They had bunk beds and wallpaper printed with large Model T's. But mostly what they had was blocks. Hundreds of them. They liked to construct giant cities, baseball stadiums, and freeway systems complete with tiny cars and Fisher-Price people. I'd swear that those people—spool-shaped, two inches high—multiplied at night. Over the years, windows, doors, and street addresses appeared on the blocks. The people acquired names and elaborate life stories.

My husband and I said our sons' room should be cleaned up each night. For several years when they were very small we managed to reload the toy chest and the block box and the bookshelf each night. But gradually our efforts to neaten the room lagged behind the boys' ability to undo our work.

The struggle over room cleaning took on a distinct pattern

as the clutter accumulated with ever-increasing speed. I didn't have the heart to make them deconstruct a whole days' work at bedtime. "We only had time to build it today," they'd moan. "We're going to play with it tomorrow." And then the next day they'd have new reasons for maintaining it. By bedtime I'd have been convinced: Why shouldn't they have fun? I realized my efforts at enforcing clean-up time had always lacked enthusiasm, and rightfully so. I really shouldn't care what their room looked like if they were having fun.

My husband was the one who was disturbed by long-term messes. He was happy to see the kids playing together and enjoying their room but felt one project should be put away before another was started. The boys insisted that every new building or roadway belonged to the same project. Their father could ignore the state of their room for just so long. Inevitably, the day arrived when he took charge and the boys went to work. Crumpled papers were retrieved from under the bed, torn picture books tossed out, and game pieces reorganized in their boxes, and the boys were told they could not watch television for three nights. While they cleaned, I stayed out of the way. Afterward I noticed how well the braid rug suited the room and realized that I had not seen it in weeks.

Consistency, my husband and I have always believed, makes for better child raising. The importance of a clean room was the one and only point where we diverged. Like most children, ours learned what they could get away with. They operated on the principle that guides illegal parkers: The cost of the ticket is less than the garage fees you might have paid. Our sons' motto might read: The punishment received for a messy room is less painful than the task of keeping it clean.

As the boys grew older they longed for privacy. Who could blame them? I had my office to hide in; my husband had the right to close himself up with music in the den whenever he chose. They were stuck with each other. Giving them their own rooms was one of our major reasons for moving.

Now that each boy can make his own messes, our older son

acts on the following principle: If you can't see it, then it must not be bad. He drops magazines he's finished reading into the space between his bed and the wall. His dresser has no special drawers for different clothes. Socks mix with balled-up shirts; shorts bed down with musty flannel pajamas. He stores dirty socks inside his closet. He can never find anything without a search.

Our younger son operates on another principle, creating visible havoc like a hurricane. His clothes fall to the floor where he undresses; school papers slide over his desk in dangerous piles. The top of his dresser provides storage for unrelated, highly valuable items: camera, deodorant, an empty soda can, scrunched-up dollar bills. Yet he finds just what he needs exactly where he left it, as easily as a librarian locates a book using a catalog number.

Occasionally I suffer for my lack of vigilance. The other day when the electrician came I moved my oldest son's bed away from the wall, revealing an incredible collection of "stuff." I struggled with an embarrassed need to say something that would exonerate me from blame. Before I could make my usual speech about kids being kids, the electrician kicked aside some balled-up socks and got to work.

In a couple of years both sons will be away at college. Until then I'll go on not caring about their rooms and my husband will continue to insist on intermittent clean-ups. He figures that eventually his standards will take hold. I figure when the kids leave home I'll shovel out their rooms.

Drawer Liners

LAURA GREEN

There used to be so many little things I considered to be, if not precisely signs of a well-run house, then signs of a cared-about one, indicators that a woman appreciated the finer points, the rewarding little frills of housekeeping. Drawer liners, for instance, are the little white gloves of housekeeping. I found one the other day wadded up on top of some toy bears in my son's bedroom. There it was, little blue flowers and all, a rectangle of quilted plastic-covered cotton that was supposed to be sprinkled with cologne. I had lined the drawers at some earlier point, long before I put the dresser in his room, long before we had this house, long before my son, now ten, was born. His other two drawers probably still have little blue flowers underneath the sweatpants and hockey socks; they just haven't come unmoored yet.

There once was a time when I folded my clothes neatly, right down to the underwear. The stockings went in stocking bags, the gloves—I still wore thin leather gloves then—in a glove box. I would never have put my underwear down on bare wood. Some fussy place in me recoiled at the idea of a tiny splinter running a stocking.

The whole thing is a moot point, really, although many dresser drawers in my house still are lined with paper—to what end, I'm no longer certain. I rarely wear stockings and I lost the stocking bags during some move or other. Stockings now go in two characterless bags in the closet—one for clean ones, one for the dirty ones, which go into the washing machine when I have enough.

I learned housekeeping in another world, one where the mothers I knew were more likely to be telling someone how to scrub than scrubbing themselves. It was a fussy life, I suppose, for women who did not have enough to do to fill their days. The minutiae of housekeeping have gone out the window. They are no longer raisons d'être. We are busy, we are working—though we do more drawer lining at the office than we care to acknowledge.

Could that really have been me, a woman who can't find anything in the clutter, who used to put paper liners between the good dishes? Who owned engraved stationery? (Now I telephone.) Who cooked multicourse meals? That woman is gone. In her place is a frazzled, middle-aged professor with children she loves deeply, challenging work, and days so full she sometimes forgets what she came into a room for.

Considering everything I gained, I made out like a bandit.

Collecting

CARROLL STONER

It's hard to understand people who don't collect things, who don't surround themselves with things they have chosen to love.

That's not quite right. What is difficult to understand is why they worry about being judged by others if they declare their tastes. That, after all, is what collecting is all about.

As a child, I learned about good old things by accident. My adopted grandfather, a very old man who had lost the attention of those close to him with his stories, loved to recall the last of the Indian uprisings in Minnesota. I was not bored by his tales. To encourage me to sit still, he would take out his collection of small bronze dinosaurs and let me hold them and play with them while he talked. They were darkened with age, though the tips of the ears and tails still gleamed. They were heavy and cold in my hand, and when I held them and listened to him, they became all things old and exotic and strange. At the age of four, I pictured the Indian wars with dinosaurs and buffalo on the plains of southern Minnesota. It took me years to straighten things out, if I ever really did.

My grandfather's apartment was filled with curios and fine possessions, including a cookbook that dated back to the turn of the century. It was the first book I loved. One section was recipes and another, the good part, was filled with advice for housewives—such as never iron your husband's underwear during the first glowing years of marriage, lest he be spoiled forever. Grandpa Riedel was forever tied in my mind to union suits and cake recipes, with dinosaurs and wild Indians in the background.

Many years later, at a church rummage sale, I saw a similar book and eagerly paid the 25 cents it cost. Now, I give it to my favorite people when we're sitting around my table after dinner, and I like them more if they read it as greedily as I did as a young girl.

I value my possessions—sometimes too much, I think. They all have meaning. It is said that objects slip into the background when they're in a home for many years, that time makes it difficult to separate them from their surroundings. I have my share of forgettable, nearly invisible possessions. But often, when I look at things I have collected, I recall details of their purchase or some event linked to them.

My ceramic pitchers are of no particular era or design, but they cover a tabletop and make useful containers for Christmas pine boughs, flowers, party wine, or juice at breakfast. Every time I pass that table, I gloat a little and want to reach out and pat my favorite on its smooth, round bottom.

My father started my collection of blue-and-white porcelains, although they can't really be called porcelains—it sounds too fancy. What they are is blue-and-white dishes: plates and platters and jars and vases that I look for at garage sales and antique shops and here and there. They look wonderful lined up on shelves and I love them out of all proportion to their value.

I started this collection by accident, which is how the best collections start, when I was living in Mexico. My father came for a visit, and together we grieved over the recent death of my mother. Showing him my adopted country was a bittersweet experience, since we both wished we were a family instead of a widower and his daughter.

Sharing a meal overlooking the beautiful Bay of Acapulco, my father told me he loved me and said I was like the last rose of summer, like my mother. He didn't explain what he meant, and I couldn't ask. But he gave me a glimpse of the sentiment that only my mother had seen. A few days later we saw a special hand-painted blue-and-white ceramic called Puebla Talavera ware. The cheerful design of curves surrounding a single bird spoke to both of us. I was single, but like my dad a born nester, so when he offered to buy me a set of those dishes, expensive even two decades ago, I was touched.

Over the next years, in and out of a bad marriage and living in five different cities in as many years, I carefully packed and unpacked my dishes. Wherever I was, and however dire the circumstances, my Mexican dishes meant home. They still do. I have finer pieces than the few primitive hand-painted blue-and-white plates that survived. But none is closer to my heart.

That's what collections are. They're the layers of life that recall memories and experience, held carefully within the four walls of our homes to welcome us like old friends. Collections tell us about ourselves. They can reveal personal traits we have not articulated, like the mixed feelings we have toward simplicity or high standards, or a hidden taste for history.

I have always loved paraphernalia linked to my father's dairy business, which he loved and lost sometime between the Depression and the time I was born. Years after I began to collect antique butter churns I understood that I was probably buying them to live up to my memories of him. They reminded me that he thought the trend toward margarine bespoke something dire in America—a general lowering of standards.

"Who would eat that stuff if they could get butter?" he used to ask.

Not I, Dad.

Pack Rats

JANICE ROSENBERG

When my aunt moved, she spent weeks looking through what some people would callously call her "junk." When her accumulations were brought up from her apartment building's basement storage space, they covered most of the living room floor. She had saved, among other things, all the receipts from her son's 1952 bar mitzvah, a newspaper clipping announcing my father's graduation from medical school in 1938, all the letters that my four cousins wrote to her in all the years they went to camp, and countless photographs, books, and notebooks going back to her own high school days. The extent of her saving qualified her as a first-class pack rat. However, my

aunt should not be seen as just some slob who can't be bothered to take out the garbage. She excels at housekeeping: no
dust balls hide beneath her dining table; no clothing dangles
over the bedroom chair. Her kitchen sparkles. Possessions
she's saved have been preserved as carefully as stamps in a
philatelist's book.

It must be in the genes. Only my mother's sharp eye has
prevented my father from competing with his sister's volume
of accumulations. For years my father saved medical journals.
At the end of each year he stacked them, tied them with
twine, and stored them in the basement. Every three years or
so he lugged them to a bindery, no matter that he hadn't
looked at any of them since the first read-through. He insisted
he would be more likely to refer to them if they were placed
between hard covers.

After a decade, as shelf space was depleted, he gave up
binding, but he could not deny himself the pleasure of stacking and storing. Eventually he donated these valuable resources to his hospital's library. If this gift duplicated the
library's back numbers, the librarian had the kindness not to
say so—and the discretion to wait until he left to throw them
out.

Journals aren't my father's only weakness. For years after
World War II was over, he kept his army sleeping bag and
mess kit—just in case. Or maybe he kept them for sentimental
reasons, to remind him of his wonderful days in New Guinea,
swatting mosquitoes, playing endless games of bridge and
watching sergeants catch fish for supper by blasting tidal pools
with hand grenades. In New Guinea he created table lamps
from coconut shells. For years my brother and I used them in
the bedroom that we shared.

In the area of accumulations, I take after my mother, who is
not a real saver. But even she has always kept one kitchen
drawer for odds and ends. As a child I searched it often to see
what new item had been thrown in, expecting pirate gold but
satisfied to find a charm from a bubble gum machine or a short

length of indelible pencil. I promote this disorganized drawer tradition in my home, too. The kitchen junk drawer is the perfect place to save odd nuts and bolts (always needed the day after they're thrown away), search for a length of string, or discover a gummed picture hook. In that drawer I keep rubber bands rescued from bunches of broccoli or from the morning paper. But unlike my brother-in-law, a confirmed pack rat, I do not feel obliged to save each one that comes my way. (His obsession has made him the proud owner of a rubber-band ball six inches in diameter).

Pack rats work on the following principle: You never know when you might need it. They love being able to say "See? Aren't you glad I saved it?" when the button on the window sill turns out to be the one lost six months earlier from your summer jacket. They make no effort to display their keepings on special shelves or use them as dinner party centerpieces. Just knowing they are available is pleasure in itself.

And pack rats savor small economies. At birthday parties, my aunt requested that we unwrap our presents carefully. She smoothed the paper and reused it. I would ascribe most of these habits to growing up poor if my own comfortably raised teenaged son had not inherited them as well. Several worn-out, ill-fitting pairs of tennis shoes stand carefully boxed on his closet shelf. Books he may want to reread "someday" wait under his bed. Shirts that will never fit again stick out from his dresser drawers. Pictures crayoned in kindergarten fill his desk. It's as if everything he touches somehow becomes a part of him, as indispensable as an arm or leg.

When we stay in motels my son manages to make one section of the room into a pack-rat haven within a day or two. He corrals local newspapers, comics that come with bubble gum, and brochures describing every local site from rock museums to Flintstone amusement parks. It's not that he's too lazy to find the trash. According to him, these items are not trash. You can never tell when you might want to know the hours for the snake museum and monkey jungle.

Pack rats delight in surprising someone by having just what's needed. I can empathize because I carry a Swiss Army knife in my purse for just that reason. However, this habit should not be misconstrued as the sign of a pack rat. I made a conscious decision to carry the knife for purely practical reasons. It gives me a feeling of independence and reliability. More than once I've whipped it out, pleased with my own resourcefulness, to slice cheese at a picnic or tighten a bicycle screw. It rests just below my wallet in the back section of my small purse, the contents of which I monitor as carefully as an army ordnance officer.

My college roommate used a satchel bigger than a mail carrier's bag. She called the thing her "pocketbook"—a contradiction in terms as far as I could see—and she dragged it everywhere. If anyone needed a safety pin, give her a minute (or fifteen) and she just might find one. Each night before going to bed she loaded her bag with valuable possessions such as the notes from physics lab; if the dorm caught fire she planned to leave with everything in hand.

While my roommate's motives were reasonable, her methods lacked an organizing principle. One day, determined to clean the bag, she dumped its contents on her bed. In the jumble she was pleased to find a barrette labled missing, weeks earlier, disgusted to consider the number of candy wrappers, appalled to see an unmailed birthday card now three months late, delighted to find a handful of pistachio nuts (which we shared), irritated to discover the snapshot of a boyfriend long since dropped and ultimately enriched by three dollars and seventy-six cents in change. I myself was glad to retrieve my Parker T-ball Jotter, lent in an emergency and soon given up as lost.

In a similar fashion, my husband is a pocket pack rat. He extols this practice each time he finds an unexpected cache of money in his raincoat. When he puts on a suit he has not worn for some time, he enjoys deciphering ticket stubs and reminiscing about the performances they represent. When emptying the pockets of his winter coat for its annual trip to the dry cleaner, he discovers a battery for his pager. A working battery? Who knows? People in their right minds don't save used ones, but pack rats are a little off. Lots of tissues, of course. A small key that no one recognizes. A roll of exposed film. (So that's where it's been since our vacation.) A stick of gum. A ballpoint pen. (Once again my ballpoint pen. *Never* make loans to a pack rat, I remind myself.)

On the other hand, a pack rat never loses anything. My husband hasn't lost his gloves, he tells me one sub-zero night. He just can't find them. They'll turn up somewhere, perhaps in the tangle of scarves and hats on the closet shelf in the front hall. Or maybe in his car trunk with an overdue library book (what other kind is there?) and a gift-wrapped Christmas box of Fannie Farmer candy—in July, of course.

A true pack rat sits in vigilance, with his attic and basement bulging, waiting for the inevitable challenge from someone less acquisitive. In my aunt's case the perpetrator was her daughter, arriving from New York to help with the move. During their week together, weeding through the contents of the living room, they had a wonderful time, full of serendipitous moments, laughter, tears, and memories. But despite these pleasures the fact remained that my aunt could not move all this old stuff to her new apartment. And so the sorting began.

My aunt now lives in a brand-new, glass-walled high-rise apartment with more closet space than she has ever had. Maybe that's some consolation for the boxes that she left behind.

Gadgets

LAURA GREEN

I look at people's gadgets with about as much tolerance and open-mindedness as I look at their politics. I like them or I don't. With kitchen gadgets, mostly I don't.

Live in Chicago long enough and Mies van der Rohe rubs off in a big way, even on little things. As he said, form ought to follow function. And though he was too busy designing high-rises to give much thought to the lemon zester, his dictum makes as much sense in the kitchen as it does on the boulevard. Unfortunately, in the kitchen, as in life, form follows function about as often as a cow follows a straight line. Most kitchen gadgets are designed for people with more cupboard space than sense.

Although you don't find much of it around, simplicity is what works in the kitchen. Take a pot, for example, or a pitcher. It would be hard to find something better to pull the cap off a bottle than a plain metal beer cap lifter. In the interests of honesty, however, I admit to owning a heavy brass one shaped like the front view of a moose, a gift from my son on a trip to Toronto. You pull the cap off by hooking it between the antlers, and to tell the truth, the thing is so ugly it is endearing. More to the point, no one messed with the basic function, which is why we still have it around. On a more Miesian note, a toothpick is a near-perfect gadget. So is a kitchen match or a slotted spoon. A plastic deviled egg carrier with a detachable handle just isn't in the same league.

The ideal gadget is small and simple and does more than one thing. But since life is not ideal and I am not an autocrat like Mies, I own a few kitchen tools that can only do one thing. I like them because they do that one thing well. The strawberry huller is not necessary, but it's easier than a knife and kinder on the thumb than using your fingers. Rube Goldberg's heirs probably hold the patent on the cherry pitter, but it does the job. It's so silly-looking that when my children were little, they fought for a chance to pop the pits out of the cherries when I happened to be fast enough to get the fruit off the trees before the birds did. The cheese grater that looks like a scale model of a space probe is the best gadget for flaking Parmesan onto a plate of pasta. Apple corers, garlic presses, and melon ballers all justify the space they take up in the drawer because they work better than a kitchen knife. Any gadget that doesn't do the job better than something simpler ought to go out with the trash.

Of course, as anyone who didn't get the engineering degree required to make cappuccino in a gleaming cappuccino maker knows, bad gadgets come in large sizes, too. A bread-baking machine turns out a loaf that's shaped all wrong, like a squared-off coffee can, and does violence to our primal notions of bread. Cordless electric can openers are too finicky. To get them to run, you have to position them just so along the edge of the can, push the button, and hope for the best. It would be quicker and easier to open the can by jumping onto it from a chair. A three-inch-long manual can opener does a much better job and you don't have to drill holes in the wall to hang it up.

The cordless can opener stands for the whole gadget problem. Expensive, cumbersome, ugly, electrified, inflexible, and inefficient, it flies in the face of common sense. A gadget is supposed to make work easier. It shouldn't have too many parts, take up a lot of space, require a storage case, or come with an instruction manual.

How we got to this pass, I do not know. Once I would have argued that men were putting something over on women, but if anything, men are even more drawn to silly gadgets than women are. My husband once came home from a garage sale beaming. He had just bought an automatic dog-water dispenser. It was big, ugly, and blue. All we had to do was put a jumbo-sized plastic soft drink bottle filled with water upside down in it, he said, and the water would dribble into the bowl as the dog needed it. The fact that the dog already had a water dish that had been supplying water on demand for years without fuss was irrelevant. After the kind of energetically stupid argument that only a couple who have been together for a long time can have, I washed the metal dog dish and put it away in the pantry. My husband proudly assembled the new dog-watering system. He filled it with water, set it down, stood back, and watched a quart of water pour all over the kitchen floor.

I don't want to sound like an old peasant sniffing at newfangled notions of electricity and running water, but good gadgets are good tools and therefore are worth insisting upon. It is a matter of self-respect. When you take work seriously, you take the tools seriously, too. When you don't, you wind up with a wet floor and a wife who's laughing so hard she can't stand up.

Money

MARY BETH DANIELSON

Two days ago I broke down and cried. I stood sobbing at the kitchen sink, drenching my T-shirt with my own tears, blowing my nose into paper towels. My alarmed husband came to my side. "What's wrong?" he said.

"I'm paying the bills and I don't know how to use the memo field on the computer check-writing program," I said.

People philosophize about how relationships should be. How they manage their money reveals how things truly are.

In the depths of the Depression, Grandpa Anderson ran a grocery store and Grandma ran their apartment upstairs over the store. If she needed groceries for dinner, she'd send one of the children down the back steps. They'd get the items, tell Grandpa, then carry them up to her. She rarely bought anything else and consequently never carried money. When she went to Ladies' Aid at church, she'd stop at the store first to get 15 cents for the collection.

The bane of her modest existence was Sunday night. Grandpa was church treasurer, and the bank's deposit slot was not open at night, so Grandpa had to bring the evening offering home. Grandma could barely sleep. She must have expected armed robbers to break into their apartment and steal the few dollars in loose change that were zipped shut in a bank deposit bag and hidden in the back of a kitchen cupboard.

I think of her often. I think of the luxury it would be to

have no responsibility to understand or untangle family finances. Her job was to be frugal and she did that beautifully.
Grandpa's job was to run the store, and he never told Grandma
how close they were to losing it. While she fretted over the
church collection in the cupboard, he prayed to God that
the business would make it through one more month, that the
Depression would end, that the people in the neighborhood
would pay their tabs before he went under. Forty years later
he told my mother about the experience of living with so much
fear.

For about a year and a half I was a credit collector at one of
America's classiest department stores. I discovered that the
rich have just as many problems with their money as the rest
of us and sometimes more.

New files came across my desk every morning, and a glance
at each usually told me the story. A couple may have been in
the collection department eight or nine times before. Perhaps
they lived in one of this area's wealthiest suburbs, or in a
luxury high-rise apartment building. Occasionally they made
single payments on their accounts that reached into the thou-
sands of dollars, which showed that when they were moti-
vated, they could find the resources to pay their bills.

What startled me was how often it sounded as if the people
in those families hated each other. Sometimes I'd hear about
"that bastard's affair," and how she responded by buying more
clothes for herself. Or that he was angry at her and tried to bar
her as a buyer on "his" account. The fireworks of exploding
marriages went off in the front office. Teenagers would charge
hundred-dollar lunches at the store restaurants and the parents
would object to paying the bill, angrily blaming the store
because their seventeen-year-old was out of control.

I'd politely agree they didn't need to pay for the $14,000
dining table that was delivered with a scratch until it was
fixed. But I marveled that people would choose such furniture
in the first place. Were they planning to arrange their lives so
the furniture would receive no more nicks? If they have museum-

quality furnishings, do they live in museums? Is that why their children spend money carelessly? Is it the only way they can get their parents' attention? The anger at home came through the files on my desk.

People in "traditional" marriages intrigue me. He makes the money, he pays the bills, he tells her how much she can spend. I watch to see if that type of family is calmer, if there is less anxiety in it.

Not at Lotta and Mark's. He is fairly successful, makes an adequate salary, and isn't in danger of losing his job. Six months ago he received a raise. Only a few weeks later she sighed and said she wished he'd make a new budget to go with the new income level. But couldn't she just figure that out herself?

"Sure, I could do it. But if I do, and the fit isn't comfortable, he'll get peeved, so I always wait for him. Although then I worry we are spending it on the wrong things, that we aren't saving enough."

Money is power. It rests uneasily in marriage. He buys a $40 tie and no one questions him—that's dressing for his career. She spends $40 on a new purse and he "kids" her about spending all "his" money on clothes. She does the weekly shopping at the grocery store and no one blinks if there's a few extra treats in the bags. He does the same thing and gets teased about artichoke hearts for months.

There's a bonus from work. One spouse wants to fly to a resort, the other wants to put the money in the childrens' college fund. There is no Solomon around, marriages fray at the edges, and sometimes they rip down the middle.

In the long run my husband and I are okay. (It's my essay, after all.) We take shifts of financial responsibility. I'm on for six months, then he does the work for six months. Each year we get a taste of the agony and the ecstasy of being in charge. It sounds good; it works; it's egalitarian. So why was I sobbing at the sink?

Because no matter what the system, it's a struggle. For the

last half year my husband has run his business out of our home and we're both tired of it. We're tired of his not getting a regular paycheck. We're tired of juggling constant bills and inconsistent payments from clients. On that day at the sink, I could see that it wasn't going to work; we were going to get behind on some of the bills. I wanted to smash something, but what I did was cry.

I heard the results of a survey that shows that most Americans, no matter what their income level, think life would be fine if they just earned 15 percent more money than they do.

We all know that on a global scale, we Americans are rich. We have food, safe water, cars, and homes. We have blue jeans, glamour magazines, and television. But what we know doesn't seem to change how it feels.

Crises can come from left field and knock us nearly out of the game. For us, it happened when my husband's employer went out of business with no warning. For others it may be layoffs, medical disasters, or sky-rocketing taxes on property that was a modest value twenty years ago. Public school education may not be what we want for our children, but private education is going to strap us for life.

There's panic and guilt in such situations. With all our careful economies—tuna casseroles, discount toiletries, purchasing a car that cost $10,000 less than the one we really wanted—shouldn't things be easier? The wife returns to work after the new baby earlier than either spouse really wants, but there's still no sigh of relief.

All I can imagine is that money isn't just an individual problem. The nation's off-balance economic situation affects our private lives. Debt-ridden capitalism doesn't breed contentment. We choke on it. I imagine that my grandparents choked on it, too. My grandmother told herself she hated the Sunday evening collection, but she wasn't stupid. She knew what was happening to small businesses in the Depression.

My traditional friends choke on it, too. The women rarely sit down; they work in their homes like undocumented work-

ers in cabbage fields. Under their docility lies anxiety. They
scrub harder, clip more coupons, yell at the children.

My husband and I make dark jokes about financial security.
We drink too much coffee and the computers in this house tap
from six in the morning until midnight. We bought a second
car with a down payment made from our temporarily paid-off
Visa card. I often tuck the kids in the back seat of our
cheap, egg-shaped car and cart them away to the best the city
has to offer, in spite of our financial insecurity.

I take them to Marshall Field's for lunch in the Walnut
Room. They eat hot dogs; I eat chicken salad in a crisp potato
basket; they eat my peaches and finger sandwiches. They love
to drink the water out of the heavy goblets. I order the
decorated children's ice cream sundaes for their dessert, drink
my coffee, and watch their happy faces. The lunch costs $25.
I pay it defiantly. We have a good time.

FRESH
STARTS

Baggage

JANICE ROSENBERG

His mother's meatballs were as big as a pair of his father's rolled-up socks. My mother's were strictly marble-sized, more suitable for toothpicks than sinking ships. His parents held a weekly Sunday afternoon cocktail hour complete with sprats on seatoast, two things I'd never heard of, let alone eaten. At my house on Sunday afternoons, depending on the weather, we either grilled hotdogs outdoors or roasted them in the fireplace in our recreation room. His mother dressed in skirts and stockings to do the marketing, while mine wore slacks. His father put on a tie and suit coat to go out and buy the newspaper. Mine allowed the neighbors to see him raking leaves in an undershirt and Bermuda shorts. As a teenager, my fiancé was expected to earn his own pocket money. I was simply handed whatever I needed.

Despite the differences in our families' styles, Michael and I got married. To our credit, we had certain larger issues in common: we were both Jewish college grads, born in the postwar baby boom, determined to have a good marriage and raise a family of our own. We moved into our first apartment unaware of our stubborn, dogmatic loyalty to our families' unexamined ways of life and the part it would play in our future.

In the house where I grew up, rules abounded. My mother insisted that clothing on all hangers in all closets face in one direction, like worshippers with their eyes on Mecca. She insisted that we always return the milk carton to the left-hand side of the refrigerator's top shelf and cut pats of butter from only one end of the stick. My father wore his suits in a rotation system set up to accommodate some inner rhythm incomprehensible to outsiders. When I helped him wrap Christmas presents for his office personnel, I found myself struggling without success to cut the Scotch tape to the exact length pictured somewhere in his brain or fold the paper ends into the perfect pointed triangles he considered correct.

Growing up, I accepted my parent's dictates without thinking, and Michael accepted just as readily his own parent's behavior. In the bathroom of his youth, various brands of toothpaste and soap appeared at random, brought home from his father's pharmacy. Such a lack of brand loyalty seemed blasphemous to me. Raised on the dependable aroma of Camay soap and the minty flavor of Crest, I balked at sandalwood and imported French tooth powders. Random housekeeping made me nervous. His mother did the laundry whenever the hamper overflowed. She measured flour for homemade noodles by handfuls and salt by pinches, then cut the dough into odd-sized lots. Cucumbers for salad might be chunks or slices, depending on her mood.

Before we married, it never occurred to me that I'd inherited by osmosis my parents' predilection for creating and following rules. In our new home Michael began questioning these tendencies. He was as devoted to chaos as I was to order. We held long debates on whether doing morning bathroom chores in an unchanging order freed your mind for higher contemplation, or merely revealed an inflexible rigidity. Did having separate dresser drawers for various clothing items save invaluable hours over the course of a lifetime, or did it cloak a terrified refusal to accept the inevitable randomness of the universe? Did watering the plants each Saturday NO MATTER WHAT free you from thinking about them during the rest of the week or imply an inability to rearrange schedules according to need?

He called me compulsive. I accused him of being purposefully uncompulsive and pointed out that the results were far from self-serving. I saw necessity and logic behind my rules. He saw only what he called a determination to assert my will. When I found the measuring spoons in the paper-and-pencil drawer, or a cookbook out of line on the shelf, I berated him for his childish refusal to support my righteous belief in the comforting quality of order. When I closed the book he'd left face down on the couch and set in on the end table with an appropriate bookmark, he accused me of undermining the basic pleasures of his arbitrary existence.

For years this was our dialectic. Had we been Democrat and Republican, Darwinite and Creationist, rigid Communist and dogged capitalist, our fights could not have been more bitter. We concurred on large issues—we wanted the United States to stay out of other countries' wars, knew we'd never move to the suburbs, chose ski vacations over lazing in the Bahamas, and as time passed, raised our children with unfashionable strictness. But we could not agree on whether shoes should be stored beneath the bed.

Why did it matter so much?

In the beginning I truly believed that my way of hanging pictures, washing floors, or driving from our house to our destination was the one and only right way. For his part, Michael didn't need to be right. He simply did not want me to tell him that he was wrong. He chafed at rules, refused to be controlled, interpreted my advice as bossiness, and never considered whether following it might benefit him.

Professing mutual love and sympathy, we pretended to be helpmates while we secretly became adversaries. When I suggested that he take a jacket to the Cubs game and reminded him of the chilly shadows in the upper deck, he insisted that the day was warm. Watching him shiver through the ballgame's final innings, I gloated triumphantly. He thumbed his nose at me by proving that it took the same number of minutes to reach a mall by taking Lake Shore Drive as it did by going on the Kennedy Expressway. Using our family styles as cover, we counted up new points in an ongoing undercover power struggle.

One important consideration in the matter of style held true for both our families: Our fathers ruled. They chose vacation spots and new cars, made final decisions about synagogue affiliation and children's education, determined what could be spent for a new sofa or a restaurant dinner. Our mothers might murmur protests in the kitchen to sympathetic children, but in the end they knuckled under. By holding sway over domestic matters, however, they got their own back. Michael's mother served his father lamb stew for years, and claimed not to have known of his distaste each time when he protested that he hated it. My mother, although an expert at ironing frilly dresses, pressed my father's shirts so poorly that finally he suggested using the Chinese laundry.

While our parent's arrangements had worked for them, they did not work for us. The part of Michael that respected my opinions and relied on my commonsense advice fought the part that would be king. He feared that given an inch I would take charge and make him the kind of henpecked husband that his father ridiculed. As for me, while I had outwardly accepted the position of dependent wife, it did not suit my independent personality, and in compensation I clung grimly to being right in small things.

It would be nice to say here that we awoke one morning changed, to report that overnight I learned to express my real needs and that he learned to accept my desire for equality. It would be nice to claim that I released my grip on "my way" without a terrible inner struggle and that he did not mourn his era of being sun to my planet. Nice, but hardly true. After fifteen years, despite the views we held in common and the love with which we'd started, we faced a growing inability to live together peacefully. This recognition led to months of intense conversation complete with outside help.

Marriage counseling does wonders for couples like us. We still had moments of deep affection and, underneath our antagonism, longed to be happy together. In the therapist's office we felt safe showing our anger and admitting our fears. Like any other "Can This Marriage Be Saved?" pair, we learned how to communicate honestly. Without undergoing psychoanalysis, we investigated the various "parts" of ourselves that made us act the way we did. Better still, we learned how to use and control these parts to benefit our relationship. We grew in understanding of ourselves and of each other.

This complicated process took almost a year. We've continued on our own since then. Every Sunday morning the two of us meet at the kitchen table for second cups of coffee and conversation. We've discussed Michael's habit of leaving his sunglasses on the kitchen counter for days, my tendency toward bossiness, his occasional offhand treatment of my work, our worries about the kids' school problems. Our months with the therapist taught us how to keep accusation out of our voices, how to take criticism, how to accept being wrong, how to forgive.

And now? When he tries out endless brands of shaving cream "just like his father" or I neatly fold my dirty clothes on my side of the suitcase "just like my mother," we laugh and say the apple never falls far from the tree. Our power struggle is over and we have deciphered from the jumble of our baggage a basic style that is all our own.

The New Lamp

MARY BETH DANIELSON

For too long, one of the most dubious items in our house was a defiantly tacky floor lamp. It started its life somewhere in the astro-inspired fifties. In fact, it looked a lot like a satellite sitting on a pole. It came into our life via my husband's sister, who purchased it for $4 at a resale shop. She took it home and painstakingly wrapped the entire thing in jute twine. The twine probably cost more than the lamp.

My husband's sister is no fool. When she and my husband split up housekeeping, she made him take the lamp. Enter me. After only a few weeks of dating I began to realize I might spend the rest of my life with this man. It never occurred to me that I might also spend the rest of my life with that lamp.

We married. For the next seven years that lamp stood at tacky attention next to our sofa. It shed light over innumerable novels, parties, late-night TV, late-night romance, then late-night nursings of our babies. Occasionally it would droop some loops of jute. It'd tuck them back up and that was that. The lamp always worked, and that meant it stayed.

Then one spring my husband was given a new stereo system as a work bonus. It is a beautiful, powerful piece of black and glass equipment. Bruce Springsteen turned to volume setting six (the control goes up to twelve) sends the dog running to the back door. "Appalachian Spring" played on the CD player gently rocks the whole house.

It took a whole day to carry seven boxes of complex stereo components into the house and hook them up. That evening we put on the first record and innocently turned the volume to twelve. Both children woke instantaneously, our neighbors' lights went on in a flash, and ours dimmed. We leapt up, spun down the volume and ran to comfort the kids. When we returned to the living room we started laughing. Quietly and undramatically, the lamp was coming undone. The shade was half exposed. It was too late to fix it; we sat and watched for fifteen minutes as that jute unlooped and puddled onto the floor. When the show was over, we picked the thing up and carted it out to the trash.

For years I had been scanning Sunday supplements for floor lamp sales. I looked at them in store windows as I walked past. I coveted other people's lamps. I worried that my passion for floor lamps stemmed from rampant materialism in my heart.

The day after the stereo debacle, I went to a furniture store and bought a new lamp. It is skinny and black and has a simple white shade. It looks great along the same wall as the stereo.

Rehabbing a Loft

LAURIE ABRAHAM

At the party we threw to celebrate our newly rehabbed loft, my friend and lover of six years acted like a man who had just returned from war, like one who had come from a hot fear in a foreign land to a back-yard family picnic. Paul usually speaks slowly and thoughtfully. But that night, as he roved the run-way stretch of the loft, his words rushed out too quickly, and his shoulders seemed to shake.

"This is a great space," guest after guest exclaimed, tugging at him and me. "God, my apartment is so small. This place is incredible."

Our friends acted like a too-cheery homecoming banner strung up in the trees. "Welcome Home," they screamed, but we were not prepared for these festivities. We were shell-shocked by the war we had waged on the loft and on each other.

June

Our home is an 8-by-10-foot bedroom with a splintered floor and a small window overlooking the barren tundra of the roof of a drugstore. Paul and I come to the cavernous loft late at night, slapping through it in $1 thongs we bought to protect our feet after midnight showers. The unfinished loft has strained our muscles as well as our love. Its crumbling ceilings and walls need patching, sometimes they must be ripped out and replaced. The floors are the kind that cannot be sanded and polished to a glossy, natural wood shine; heavy layers of paint are the only solution.

But in the bedroom, we can shut the door on that hostile terrain, if only to sleep. An old blue blanket that has served at different times as tablecloth, dropcloth, and towel, is our bed. It provides little cushion between our backs and the grooved floor, but we lie down with relief and listen to the neighbors' children squeal at our doorstep until 1 A.M. On hot nights, the whirring fan blocks out the sounds of the kids, the cars, and the whining alarms that only cease when the sun begins to rise. We've never found time to take the blanket to the laundromat that is just a block away, so it is splotched with yellow and brown. I do not expect that we will soon make time, either. The dirt here is thick and relentless, and we're wallowing in it.

We've surrendered ourselves to the fine black dust that settles on the oven and to the plaster pallor of our skin, but at the same time we have become slaves to a certain perverse cleanliness. I, for example, have become the self-appointed keeper of the blanket, one of few possessions of mine not packed away in a box. I brush crumbs from it and ask Paul about the origin of each new spot; every coffee stain gnaws at me. My pillowcase is another oasis of cleanliness in our desert of dirt. Everything up to the neck can rest in dust, but my hair must be clean, according to the arbitrary rules I unconsciously fashion. Unsoiled pillowcases are an obsession; when I spotted a yellow mark on mine one night, I covered it with a clean workshirt before lying down to sleep.

Paul has his own obsession. As an artist who appreciates well-drafted paintings, he insists on parallel lines and perpendicular corners in our one-room living space. On my first day here, he asked me to zip all the pouches on my backpack, and then he leaned it upright against the wall so the lines of the closed zippers would be parallel to the floor. He occasionally complains about how capriciously the heating units were installed. They are not parallel to each other.

August

Our building is in one of those neighborhoods that is always about "to turn the corner" but never quite does. Cut off from some of Chicago's most fashionable brownstones by an eight-lane highway, it sits on one of the main thoroughfares of a neighborhood called Wicker Park. Our street is to Wicker Park what a mall is to a suburb. Sandwiched between Walgreen's Drugstore to the west and Zayre's to the east, family-run stores sell shoes, clothes, and furniture, "no money down, easy credit." Some of the retailers are Hispanic, others Korean, and a few are the Eastern Europeans who dominated the area between the time of the old rich and the new poor. "Nice Polish Lady Wanted," says a permanent sign in one shop window. It isn't the shops, though, but the shoppers who remind me of my mall-bopping days. From the bedroom, I watch girls with long, dark hair dance down Milwaukee in hot pink blouses and tight, tight black pants. Their older sisters and mothers push strollers, or clutch tiny hands and Jewel Foods bags.

It is not the kind of neighborhood where I wanted to live. I envisioned leafy oaks, Victorian frills, a trendy restaurant or two, but sometimes, I must admit, I appreciate what I never wanted. Like when Paul and I walk along the street at dusk, toward Wendy's. The merchants are beginning to lock steel grates across windows full of gold dinette sets, and the grizzled old man who sits crosslegged on a stoop a few feet from ours is selling his last few *TV Guides*. We're free, swinging along, holding hands. The blinking lights that outline the sign for Barry's Cut-Rate Drug Store don't seem so garish, and some-one's picked up the trash outside our door. I even feel proud to live here, in a "real" city neighborhood, instead of one with a sports bar on every corner.

My emigration to Wicker Park began at Sacre-Coeur. I had been traveling alone in Europe for two months when Paul joined me at the bottom of the hill that leads up to the gleaming white dome that presides over Paris. "I forgot to say what made our first night together better than I could ever have imagined," I wrote in my journal. "Paul has put a deposit on an apartment for us. He wants to live with me again."

September

Anger clings to our apartment like grease. I try but cannot seem to scrape it away.

"Paul, are you here?"

I can't see him, the loft is so big. He's probably reading *Art in America* or getting ready to play the guitar. I've worked all day at the magazine; he's not going to get a job until most of the apartment is camouflaged.

"What are you doing?"

I blew it. I had wanted to resist my need to check up on him, to make sure he had been working all day on the apartment. I vow I'll refrain from any more incriminating questions. I'll be bright, loving.

"Did you finish sanding the ceiling like you wanted to?" I ask, knowing that he hadn't. I hate him already.

"No," he says from above on the ladder.

"What happened?"

"I needed new sanding paper."

Another excuse that's not really an excuse: he had all day to buy sanding paper.

Paul hates me, too. I'm always nagging; I never appreciate the work he does, never share his dreams.

Then again, Paul has said more than once, "If it weren't for Laurie, I would never be finishing the apartment as quickly as I am." I'm always shocked to hear how gratefully he says this. He, as much as I, trusts the pattern of our relationship. Just as much as we despise it.

It is a pattern that goes back to high school. In fact, Paris only explains part of how I came to live in an unfinished loft. It really began at the end of a long table where Paul and I ate lunch alone together in high school. Over cheese crackers and Diet Coke, he'd tell me all about the submarine he was going to build. He showed me his penciled diagrams, his black books containing mysterious submarine secrets. One day, I shared his enthusiasm when a local company agreed to give him an oil tank to build his sub. It was his for free if only he would fix the spigot on another of their tanks. I feared at the time that we would sink in his submarine into Lake Erie, the Loch Ness of my imagination. No matter how scared I was, or how certain of my imminent death, I would have to go down to prove to Paul that I loved him, that I loved his dreams. My friends doubted that he would ever build a submarine. I wasn't so quick to write him off. He possessed a luminous intelligence unlike that of any other boy in school. But he never fixed the spigot.

October

"We'll be done by Halloween, easy," Paul told me today as I scraped ugly brick-red paint from the windows. I didn't answer. I watched him, across the room, whistling as he smoothed blobs of joint compound into the pocks on the walls. All I could think of was the aborted submarine project and the coach house (such a find!) without heat and water. "All I have to do is figure out the plumbing, and hook up the gas, and . . ." Paul told me when he rented the coach house for $100 a month; he ended up showering at a nearby college and eating at cheap diners.

The loft, then, has become not only a place to live but also a test of whether Paul will turn one of his truly sparkling ideas into an equally sparkling reality. And I use it to test my suspicion that Paul loves his dreams, this space, more than he loves me. "I can't stand this place," I say. "Couldn't we compromise on another apartment? Wouldn't you rather have me than this loft, if I just can't live here?"

"No. I can't leave before it's finished." And I can't leave him.

May

The opening party for the loft is over. The walls are white, the floors gray. We bought a bed and have even considered flower boxes and fuchsias. Paul and I, however, are still in the midst of rehabbing our relationship. We could not pitch our anger out the back window with the rotted boards and buckets of broken plaster. It still hangs in the air like the dust you know is there but can only see in an occasional shaft of late afternoon sunlight.

Lingering resentment never makes the pages of *Metropolitan Home*, only joy at a job well done. In those pristine pages, hearty young couples take up orange linoleum and discover walnut parquet floors. Even in the attic, they uncover fine detailing. Maybe Paul and I just took the job too far. When we didn't find any sumptuous moldings behind false walls, we kept going. Unwittingly, we peeled away the layers of self-deception on which our coupling was built. It took months of reexamining and reassessing (a late-twentieth-century phenomenon as ubiquitous as rehabbing) before we came close to deciding if our postrenovation relationship was worth salvaging. It was, at least for a while. And I am something close to grateful for the goddamned loft. It forced us to grapple with our differences before we became resigned to them. I might even call it a catalyst to bring a man who would build submarines and a woman who keeps her feet firmly planted on land closer together. The loft proved to me that Paul can make some dreams come true. And it proved to him that dreams require as much perseverance as they do black-covered books with mysterious submarine secrets.

Cooking

LAURA GREEN

Part 1: Falling in Love

My romance with cooking began when I was eighteen and my sister and I and two friends fixed sukiyaki and baked Alaska for dinner. I wouldn't plan that menu again, and my sister would be the first to remind me that the host's mother blew up when I got meringue on her kitchen ceiling. Still, everything turned out to be edible—more than edible. The evening was as formative as a first kiss. I had cooked my first meal with friends, and from that point on, an almost indecent amount of my time has been spent at a kitchen or dinner table.

For the next fifteen years, my kitchen life and my social life were synonymous. Other people played volleyball, went to the mall or to concerts. Not us. We ate out or we cooked. In the beginning we made spaghetti and meat sauce—one box of pasta, one can of tomato paste, one pound of ground round, and one packet of Lawry's spaghetti sauce mix. To this day, I can recognize the smell of it.

As a new bride, I cooked for my husband's colleagues, making one or the other of two of not-quite-done chicken dishes for a few not-quite-sober reporters. Pink at the bone poultry wasn't quite fashionable, but then neither were we.

Then, as now, we ate just off the kitchen at a big oak table we had found in a Salvation Army thrift shop for $15 and then stripped and refinished. As time went on and the marriage didn't, I lived in a series of apartments with roomy kitchens big enough for the oak table during the years I had custody of it. I was amassing a growing collection of cookbooks, which I read at night before falling asleep. At least once a week my friends and I gathered around my kitchen table to eat, drink what was then dirt-cheap California wine, and fall in and out of love.

During the pinch-penny years, we made explosive curries and stews, especially a carbonnade, a beer-and-beef stew that was hard to get the hang of; it was unpredictably tough, too sweet, or too chewy. From the dope days, I remember a Thanksgiving dinner in which the unplanned highlight of the meal was a potato dish brought over by one of the guests. It consisted of three rings of potatoes. The inner circle was made of orange sweet potatoes, the middle band was white mashed potatoes, and the outer ring was also made of mashed potatoes, dyed an intense Caribbean turquoise. We admired it. It was, after all, the kind of dish you didn't see every day. But I don't remember that we ate any of it.

Through the talk, the confessions, and the seductions, there was always food on the table and cookbooks by my bedside. I taught my first husband how to set a stylish table. He taught me how to be a patient and painstaking cook. I wove lattices for blueberry pie and never once squeezed lemon juice out of a plastic lemon. I grew my own vegetables and shopped in four markets to get exactly what I wanted. Often my sister was in the kitchen with me, chopping as we analyzed the week's goings-on. We were always talking with our mouths full.

The last time I was in New York to see her, I went straight from the airport to the cab to her kitchen, stopping only to leave my bag in the hall. We chopped, stirred, tasted, and talked. The rest of the household drifted in and out as we worked, fixing before-dinner drinks, making phone calls, and drawing up the weekend's plans. Her stepson's girlfriend pulled up a stool, fished a cherry tomato out of the salad, popped it in her mouth, and said to us, "Boy, I bet your mother must have been a fabulous cook."

We stopped, looked at each other, then gave each other permission to burst out laughing, to the embarrassment of the young woman, who thought she had said the wrong thing. Of course she had, but she had no way of knowing how wide of the mark she was. The women on my mother's side of the family were legendary bad cooks. My mother was in the middle ranks, which still meant she was awful in the kitchen. The idea of her fixing anything fabulous, was, well, inconceivable. My grandmother, my mother, and my aunt were the culinary equivalent of tone deaf and indifferent to music. Their heads were somewhere else.

Still, their standards weren't so low that they couldn't recognize others' awful dishes. My mother laughed at my aunt because she poured tomato juice over fish and baked it, a precursor of the grimmest dishes on a low-fat diet. My aunt recalled my grandmother's ketchup, which she had bottled in a

fit of patriotism during World War II. Everyone else was
canning, she must have figured, so why not she? For years
afterward, the basement shelves were lined with bottles of
brown runny ketchup speckled with tomato seeds. No one ate
it. It didn't look like anything a rational person would put on
food. People didn't eat anything she cooked if they could avoid
it. When we had to eat dinner at my grandmother's apartment,
my father always fixed himself a sandwich first. He didn't
want to be tempted to eat something he would regret in the
middle of the night.

My mother's pièce de résistance—actually the only thing she
fixed with any regularity then—were hors d'oeuvres, the likes
of which I have never seen outside our big, old kitchen.
Fixing them was a day-long process. It began with a trip to the
bakery, where we picked up her order of extra-long loaves of
tricolor bread. Each loaf was a braid of grapefruit pink, lime
green, and plain white. We stared fascinated as the baker ran
the breads through the slicer horizontally, dividing each one
into nine or ten gaudy slices. Back home, I got to be a helper.
I squirted food coloring into cream cheese, stirred it in, added
some diced lox, spread the green and pink filling on the bread,
and carefully nudged each slice into a long thin roll. I held my
breath and hoped I wouldn't tear the bread. I took the job
seriously. I carefully wrapped each roll in waxed paper, then
put it in the freezer down in the basement. The freezer came
up to my ribs and I always worried about falling into it.

Hors d'oeuvres were company food. About fifteen minutes
before the guests were due, I helped set up the tippy bridge
table. The rolls were hauled out and somewhat defrosted.
Company munched their way through salty, lox-flavored cream
cheese crystals and icy, fruit-colored bread and drank Rob
Roys, which were Scotch and ginger ale and maraschinos, or
something that nondrinkers would drink. I thought we were
the height of sophistication.

The Homeric scope of my mother's bad cooking wasn't
obvious at first, at least not to us. No one else's mother made

hors d'oeuvres, and she didn't start cooking anything else until she was in her fifties. She was a union organizer, a public figure, an activist—someone with endless responsibilities. Her head was filled with strategies, not recipes. She preferred to spend her free time reading the papers and cursing the reporting, not stirring messes in the kitchen. She was contemporary in that she never wanted to cook, never even learned, and wasn't embarrassed by her indifference. Like waxing a floor, cooking was something you could pay another person to do and that was what she did.

She did like to eat, though, so she hired a housekeeper who once had been a cook in a lumber camp. Throughout my childhood, we ate very well indeed. Jenny fixed hearty foods— big roasts and mashed potatoes and meringue-topped pies. She didn't cut corners and she didn't use mixes. She peeled potatoes, boiled them, and beat them light and fluffy with a wooden spoon. We knew that dinner was ready and it was time to wash up when we heard the hollow whap, whap, whap of the potatoes being whipped in the big ceramic mixing bowl tucked under Jenny's arm. Six-course meals fit for a lumberjack were routine at our table.

Then my father died, and my sister and I grew up and moved away. My mother was on her own, which meant that from time to time she made dinner. For years I made people cry with laughter at her well-meaning attempts. She bought those dried-up barbecued chickens that seem to revolve for days on spits in the grocery store, cut them up, poured canned ravioli over them, and called it chicken cacciatore, a deception that was almost political in its brashness and futility. On holidays, either my sister and I cooked or my mother ordered from restaurants and we picked up very good dinners in huge aluminum pans at their kitchen doors. My mother cooked like someone learning to drive in middle age. I would have felt sorry for her—except that she didn't care. Her head was still in her work.

That psychological fuel was what fired my romance with

the kitchen. Like just about everyone I knew, I decided I would not be like my mother, so I became a reporter and a serious cook. We all have some realm in which we feel confident, and the kitchen was mine.

Part II: Disillusionment

Recently my husband and I had one of our now-rare dinner parties. It was a semi-potluck, something I never used to do because I couldn't control what went on the table when others brought dishes. The guests were in their early thirties, very professional and very serious about themselves and their work. I smoked game birds and made a fresh corn salad with peppers from the garden and cilantro and corn from the farmers' market. One guest brought a tasteless, brown, squatty dessert and boasted how little fat and sugar it had. Another brought something assembled out of cans. Obviously neither is kitchen-minded. Afterward, as I was putting away the leftovers, it occurred to me that a lot of women sneer at cooking in the same way they would sneer at tatting. If you have time to master this skill, it appears, it is because your priorities are all wrong. Time should be spent on work, not food. If you are good at cooking, they seem to say, it's because you're not sharp enough to be good at something more important.

That was the craven reason I gave up cooking—it was embarrassing to be expert at something that was suddenly so trivial. But I had respectable motives, too. I more or less stopped for many of the reasons my mother never cooked as well as a few that a spurned lover would sympathize with: I was busy, which holds out the possibility of being temporary, and I was unappreciated, which doesn't. I was making complex food for people with simple appetites. They wanted burgers, but I gave them veal stew. Try it, I'd say, like someone standing in the front hall with a copy of *Guideposts*. Eventually, I had to face facts. I may have been a good cook, but I was the wrong kind of good cook. I was cooking party food when they

just wanted dinner. More and more often, I caught myself
looking around the disheveled kitchen, at the sink full of pots,
at the sunny day outside, at the books I wasn't reading, at the
kids gobbling Oreos the way my father would grab a sandwich
on the way to my grandmother's, and I wondered why I was
doing this to myself.

So I stopped. We now have burgers or salad or carryouts for
dinner. My children are happy to get fast-food chicken and
pizza. I, who used to walk through the grocery store asking in
vain if anyone wanted the baby corn or the spinach pasta or
the French olives, even once, bought mousse pie mix. My stepson
taught me to make it, and it's not as bad as I thought. Granted,
that's not saying much. Even so, if you were to cut down the
amount of milk, add a little rum, and grate some hazelnuts and
semisweet chocolate into the mixture just before it set, you
might have something.

Ultra-mousse notwithstanding, I know the romance with
food is over. But even shattered pride can't keep me from
acknowledging just how much more time I have, something
my mother knew all along. Like all intense affairs, this one
finally ended. I suppose you could say I went home to mother.

Part III: A Fool for Love

I took an out-of-town guest to the farmers' market yesterday
and came home with sacks full of food. The refrigerator is
groaning with parsnips, carrots, celery, basil, squash, eggplants, peaches, plums, and two kinds of apples.

You can go home to mother if you have to, I suppose, but
how many red-blooded women stay there very long?

Balance

CARROLL STONER

I have slowed down.

This realization comes to me one morning while I'm standing waiting for the bus that takes me to my office. As I stand there, I find myself staring at a large coat button on the ground, half wondering whom it belongs to. Then, with a shock, I realize it is my own. The reason I don't recognize it instantly is that I have never, before today, stopped to button this winter coat. And a realization slowly dawns: I button my coats lately. I take buses rather than cabs. I take time to tidy up the house before I leave in the morning—and I do this with more grace and less annoyance than I've mustered in the past. Sometimes, I even allow myself the luxury of an extra cup of coffee with Oprah, whose program comes on at nine, thus delaying my arrival at the office until nine thirty or ten. Oprah can make me laugh out loud.

I'm laughing now as I stand waiting for the bus and realize all this. But I'm also perplexed, confused. How did this slowdown occur? Have I lost the competitive edge that has always propelled me? Can I make my new business a success this way? Has this slowdown improved my family life?

I recall all the effects of those years of moving fast. The first years of my second child's life, I recently realized, passed in a kind of blur. At the time, of course, I knew I was trying to do too much. I had gone back to a job I loved and would surely have lost if I hadn't reclaimed it a few months after she was born. But that alone wasn't it. Too much else happened at the same time. We moved when she was eleven months old, and the hours and days it takes to get a home organized and running smoothly didn't exist. The sense of order I crave didn't quite happen. The housekeeper I loved got sick and died a long, painful death of cancer. Our previously peaceful son hit adolescence hard. Things changed at work, too. What had been demanding but satisfying work became overwhelming when the newspaper where I was a manager changed hands in a wrenching and public corporate acquisition. The bosses I loved left, and what followed was an almost comical game of musical chairs. Which editor did I report to? After a while, it hardly mattered.

When things were going well, there was a positive side to the overload. I was more productive than I'd ever been in my life. When my boss asked me to head a task force on new products, I was thrilled. I managed the job by getting to work in the quiet of the office between four thirty and five thirty A.M. several days a week. It was hardly a strain, since I'm a naturally early riser, I told myself. And what we accomplished, directly related to the future of our company, made all the work worthwhile.

No matter that the company soon changed hands and our work was forgotten. When I was called on to speak on the subject of the woman who has it all, as I frequently was, I told audiences that there is no alternative to the struggle of trying to balance everything—if you value achievement and also want a home life. It was a heady time.

I meant those things, too. No one in my life was going without in a major way, not even me. Sure, there were small deprivations, but I was willing to forgo a few unimportant, leisurely pleasures for the important things. My audiences listened. I convinced some of them. More important, I convinced myself. So what if I didn't watch television, the time-waster of all time? So what if I couldn't manage leisurely (or even hurried) telephone conversations with friends? Friendships that ground to a halt? These were temporary sacrifices. As soon as my children got older, I'd re-enter the rest of the world.

And I think we were happy. Our family life wasn't perfect, but we were blessed with optimism, the improvident optimism that makes you believe you can do anything if you just work hard enough at it. And so we kept working harder at everything. Looking back now, it seams bleak. But at the time, the alternatives seemed worse.

My husband said I moved at two speeds: full speed ahead or dead stop. And he was right: I was either moving fast, or I was sound asleep. There was nothing in between. If it wasn't listed on our calendar, it didn't get done. And tired doesn't begin to describe how I was feeling.

Then things went from busy to overwhelming. It wasn't the work. It was the stress: the corporate takeover that created change on top of change at any price, the unstable editor-boss who played politics and involved managers in his battles with the publisher. The woman I'd affectionately described as my wife, a housekeeper who had worked for us for over a decade, died. We had cared about each other, she and I, running my home in a kind of partnership. Now who would take care of my house and, in turn, of me?

Photos from this era tell a lot. I look exhausted, with a slump to my shoulders that any mother recognizes as a sign of emotional and physical weariness. Typically, though, I didn't slow down. I braked to a dead halt. After leaving my job, I cooked, played with my children, and decorated our apartment, all at half speed. I served elaborate meals to family and friends who laughed at the new stage I was in. I read and thought and listened to music. When I had no choice but to heal, the healing process began.

As I felt better, I began to throw myself into projects, both big and small, and they became a source of delight. We bought a country house. While I set things up inside, my husband conquered the land around us. I spent a summer with our five-year-old daughter, sitting on the edge of the pool and coaching her as she graduated from the dog paddle to the backstroke. I taught her to dive and got the best tan of my life. I lost twenty pounds while trying to get her to eat more. We painted lawn furniture; she covered an old water pump in bright red enamel. For the first time in years, I found time for myself. I read—no, I *lost* myself in books. Reading fiction, chronicles of human growth and development, helped me reflect on my own capacity for change.

In my new, more private life, I put my house in order. What I'd feared the most, what had once looked like a huge, gaping void, gave me solace. In other words, my home life healed me.

And I began to question my own values. Why had leaving the world of paid work—even for a break—looked like failure? Why had life outside the workplace looked so empty, so devoid of challenge and satisfaction?

Had I been too willing to pay a high personal price for success? And did this happen because I was from the first generation of women to move into newspaper management? Our titles might have proved that we were successes, but we felt fragile. Not once did I run into a top-level newspaper manager who had combined her work with a successful marriage and family life. Even now, twenty years later, only a few exist.

This is not to blame anyone for what happened. I should have listened to my own common sense telling me to get out, slow down, cut back, start enjoying life again. But it was a quiet voice. And I had been in love with my work for so long, had been on such a noisy adrenaline high, and was working so hard to keep my head above water that I refused to admit how things around me had changed.

I did what I know is typically female: I looked within myself for fault, accepting blame for a situation that had become impossible. I finally stopped. The chaotic, breathless world of newspapers had been a good ride that lasted almost twenty years. They were unforgettable years.

But life at home is what made me whole again.

Coffee

MARY BETH DANIELSON

I drank my first cup of coffee on a Danish farm the summer I was sixteen. I sat alone at the breakfast table, scared to be so far from home, exhausted from the long journey, and anxious about being a two-month house guest to unknown people. Alma Bjerre, the housewife of the farm, stood before me, saying something slowly in Danish.

Just then, the door behind her opened. Into the room walked the handsomest man I had ever seen. It was Peter, home from college to help on the family farm. He was six feet tall, twenty-four years old, and slim and muscular, with broad shoulders. His hair was dark and slightly wavy; his brown eyes sparkled. That morning he was whistling, but stopped when our eyes met. My heart started to pound. He smiled. Blood rushed to my head. The hotness of a blush bloomed in my face. I managed to smile back at him.

"Hello." His voice was low and merry, and with that first greeting I knew we shared a secret, though it would be years before I would know what the secret was.

"My mother says, do you want tea or coffee with your breakfast?"

I stammered that coffee would be fine. She brought two cups, and Peter sat down to drink it with me. The steamy, bitter flavor of my first coffee puckered my throat and brought tears to my eyes. I stifled the urge to screw up my face and instead asked Peter why he was whistling "If I Were a Rich Man." He asked me why the United States was in Viet Nam. I don't remember either of our answers, but I do know that I have not drunk a cup of coffee since without being faintly reminded of the lovely possibilities in being an adult.

For years after that I drank coffee out of styrofoam cups from various places along my everyday route. One can maintain a serious habit in this way. There is a kind of jumpy, revved up, mojo joy to it. I felt savvy, as if there were a *Glamour* magazine caption under me saying, "This young woman knows how and where to get what she wants." Even if all I know how to get was coffee.

My husband introduced me to revolutionary idea that coffee ought to taste good. It's easy to forget that and just go for caffeine. "But without good coffee," he insisted, "all would be darkness and chaos!"

In my twenties I scoffed at decaf coffee as the pablum of the bifocaled set. Then came the fateful night during my twenty-ninth year when I simply could not fall asleep. I tossed and turned until I finally remembered the two cups of coffee I'd drunk during the evening. It was an ominous moment. I'd drunk coffee at night for years and it had never affected me. Now it had. The realization was worse than discovering my first wrinkle. With that discovery I could hope I was getting interesting. With this I knew I was definitely getting old.

Now I am in my rapidly advancing thirties. The last time my eyes were checked the ophthalmologist informed me I was "borderline for bifocals." I went home, brewed myself a pot of decaf, and thought about it.

To save face I tell people I drink decaf for my health, thought I keep wondering about a Mark Twain story. He asks, "What if you get sick? If you have no bad habits, what are you

going to give up? You'll be like a sinking ship on a stormy sea
with nothing to throw overboard."

Coffee is a companion through long days. My mother always helped my dad in our family printing business. After he
died, she ran it with my brother. Then the army drafted Paul
and shipped him to Viet Nam, so she managed the business
by herself. I was in high school then, the only child left at
home, so I helped in the print shop after school. I sat at the
front end of the shop, doing boring, repetitive jobs in the
bindery department. Sometimes I would look down the length
of the shop toward Mom. She sat hunched over the books,
over invoice cards, over the typewriter, over something. And
always, a little to one side, was her cup of coffee, in the tan
mug with the brown flowers, or the white mug with the
turquoise squares, or the plain green diner mug. Every so
often she would pick up that mug, half-full of cold black
coffee, take a sip, and set the mug back down. There would be
a small sigh, an almost imperceptible relaxing in her shoulders,
and the crease above her eyes would soften. Sometimes she
would look up and our eyes would meet and we would smile
at each other.

Coffee is a compensation for being a grown-up. I have not
shared a cup with a tall, handsome stranger in years. Nevertheless, every morning I love that first sip that feels like tiny
Italian Christmas tree lights switching on inside me. I love
middle-of-the-day cups that are ordinary and comforting, like
brown mittens. I love fresh, hot decaf after dinner with husband and friends—the sharp taste that signals it's time for
adults to talk and laugh.

I had a reunion with Alma Bjerre a few weeks ago. We
reminisced about old times. She pulled out a family album.
There was Peter. Next to him was the tall, beautiful woman
who is his wife, and in front of them were their two sons.
Peter's in his forties now and looks like Alan Alda. I poured
myself another cup of coffee.

Closets

LAURA GREEN

When I was a little girl, my closet was a hideout, a fantasy place somewhere between my life and my dreams. It was a gateway of sorts to another world, like the wardrobe that Lucy steps through on her way from an English country house to Narnia. I dreamed there was a trapdoor to another world at the back. When I began reading C. S. Lewis's *Chronicles of Narnia* to my children, I knew exactly what Lewis was writing about. He had created the closet I always wanted but could find only in my dreams.

During the day, my closet was an ordinary human closet, and from time to time, it got too full and had to be cleaned. Clothing wasn't the problem: children don't have to throw out clothes; they outgrow them. My younger sister got everything that was too small and wore it out, and that was that. But kids amass little treasures, trinkets of one kind or another that pile up on the dresser tops and in the corners of the closet. Sequins from an old doll dress. A broken comb. Wadded-up notes from friends. When I cleaned closets, I had to tackle a stack of mementos that collected to the right of the door, stuffed in old, tan shoe boxes, stacked in tippy piles.

Throwing out clothing is one thing, an easy thing. I inherited half of my wardrobe from cousins; there was no love lost between me and a series of itchy Scotch plaid pleated skirts that came and went. Throwing out the old valentine cards,

letters from camp, drawings, doodles with boys' initials, birthday cards, handmade paper dolls, social studies papers I'd
gotten A's on, lists of all the clothes I would buy if I won a
half-hour shopping spree, (as well as lists of how many skirts I
would need for a perfect wardrobe), red maple leaves crum-
bling between sheets of waxed paper, a triple acorn from the
back yard next door, a barrette—now that was throwing out of
a much higher order. It was heartbreaking.

The truth is that we can't hold on to many things for long
without forming some sort of attachment to them. We put the
imprint of memory all over our possessions, in the same transi-
tory way that we leave footprints on the sand. Our memories
dust our belongings with a sheen of importance they could
never achieve by themselves. Like magic spells, they conjure
up recollection, revive happiness, recreate triumph, bring back
the dead, blow the trumpets, and play the song once more.
Their power to evoke the past is stronger, and often more
important, than any commonsense, commonplace urge to dust
up the place.

Those associations are why closet cleaning did, and still
does, require a cold-blooded, unsparing will. Sitting on the
wooden floor in the gloomy rear of the closet, like a magpie in
a nest filled with bits of bright-colored string and shiny scraps
of foil, I forced myself to throw away the little scraps of
memory after examining them carefully for the last time. I
read each valentine, looked at it carefully, remembered how
joyous it was to see the pile of valentines with my name on the
envelopes on my old wooden desk at school. I put them on the
throw-away pile, then took them off, read them once more,
then threw them out for good.

I threw away my drawings of queens in full-skirted gowns
and the paper dolls so like the ones my daughter makes. I
emptied the dolls' own closets, which were shoe boxes filled
with the handmade paper clothes that took so long to color and
cut. I never draw any more. I wish I had kept just one doll

and just one dress to show my daughter that mothers can also be girls.

Why did I throw those things out? I had to, I suppose, to make way for other things, primarily adolescence. But I was also convinced that getting rid of the ties to the past would toughen me up. I believed that by throwing out mementos with meaning along with the stuff that had merely accumulated, I could make myself strong. I exercised a painful sort of self-discipline, hoping to build character the way a small boy does push-ups to build muscle. The boys wanted biceps; I struggled for emotional endurance, which, for a girl headed into adolescence, was not a bad thing to have in reserve. I sat there in the closet confronting the piles of paper the way someone who hates to swallow pills looks at a morning multivitamin.

If I thought something good would come from throwing away the past it was because I was growing up and didn't want to be hampered by signs of the person I used to be. My reasons were a preview of the reasons young women often cut their ties with their families and friends and move to new cities to start careers. In their new homes, there are no parents to tell them what to do, no old friends to remind them of who they were, no neighbors to tell them when to get married and have babies, no old boyfriends who demand that they become women they don't want to be. In a new place, women are free to invent themselves, to cut all links to the expectations of the past. So it is with a newly cleaned closet. An empty closet is a blank slate—the reward for tossing away small treasures is the freedom to begin all over again.

Today, I do a different kind of throwing out, primarily of clothes I have outgrown. Memories, I now know, do not need mementos. The good ones are always there, ready to comfort us, if only we have the wit to recall them when things are bad. And the bad ones cannot easily be banished; pitch them out by day and they return in the hours before dawn that F. Scott Fitzgerald called the dark night of the soul.

Not that I consider closet cleaning a waste of time any more than I would consider taking out the trash useless effort. But after many years, I have reduced it to its original purpose—to make room—instead of using it to banish my old selves to some Narnian limbo.

Living Alone

I. LAURA GREEN

When I was in my late twenties, I was moored by little besides a lease and the possessions that filled my four-room apartment. I had no children, no husband, and no steady job, so there was no place I had to be at nine on Monday morning. Divorced, twenty-seven years old, and out of work, I had no long-term plans for paying the rent or eating. I had lots of friends but nothing you could call a stable relationship. I lived by myself, and my apartment was the only constant.

It was 1969, the loosey-goosey height of the counterculture. I had just abandoned a five-year career as a graphic designer, quitting a job at Playboy's publishing house one day to go motorcycling in Europe. I liked to tell people I quit so I wouldn't have to design "Playboy's Astrological Stock Market Guide," but I think I concocted that title as a justification for what I should have done years earlier. I knew I lacked that peculiar combination of a free-swimming imagination and anal attention to detail that marks a gifted designer. I just couldn't make a printed page look good enough, no matter what I did.

Besides, I was ready to cut ties after five years of marriage. My ex-husband and I scrupulously divided the possessions, got rid of the fancy apartment, and were trying to do something about the emotional luggage. I had been an artist because my family told me I had talent and I believed them despite the growing evidence that they were wrong. I was a wife for a whole lot of reasons that made sense on paper but not from day to day. For years I had been old before my time, the respectable owner of a townhouse, the holder of a good job, smug on the outside, jealous on the inside of people whose possessions could be stuffed in the back seat of a Volkswagen beetle. When given the chance to flee, I headed for Munich, where I was sort of a silent partner and owner of a big black motorcycle. My former husband was the co-owner, which says what needs to be said about the ambivalence of divorce. I was the passenger and, therefore, a nonvoting stockholder.

For several months, I tootled around on the back of the bike, which was what I should have done years before. When I came back from Europe, I moved into a small, fortuitously cheap apartment in an old Chicago brownstone, eked out a living pasting up little magazines, and freelanced for the Chicago newspapers. I'd had a bellyful of responsibility and wanted some time to regress and regroup. The times encouraged that kind of tearing down and building up.

I started with my schedule. It didn't take long before I realized I had been a night person living on the day shift. After having gotten up on the wrong side of the bed at seven thirty in the morning for twenty-seven years, I realized a person could wake up slow and easy. It was liberating to take my shower after the rest of the world had gone to work. Finally free to drift into my own schedule, I slept until nine thirty, stumbled around in a fog until noon, settled down to work a bit later, and didn't straighten up my drawing board until one or two in the morning. Looking out at dark houses in which everyone was asleep, I knew that my window was the only one still squared off in lamplight. I felt like the narrator of a novel, as if I could look deep into those windows and know what was going on in the unguarded hearts of the people sleeping there.

Even allowing for my odd hours, learning to sleep in an otherwise empty apartment took some getting used to. Living in an absolutely quiet place for the first time was a novelty. There were no dogs scratching and thumping, no father snoring, no traffic roaring. I read until the book fell onto the blanket. When I couldn't sleep, I did my paste-ups. I rehung the posters, sewed, tried to scrub a hundred years of kitchen grease from the porcelain pores of my worn kitchen sink at midnight. I could do that without having to explain why: one of the blessings of living alone is not having to justify your behavior to an understandably anxious roommate, not even when it might be good to examine what is going on and why you don't think the hours you are keeping might be a bit strange.

Living alone gave me a chance to let my crotchets out. I played country rock nonstop. I decorated with alley salvage furniture. For nearly a year, I ate brown rice with stir-fried vegetables, soy sauce, and a few rubbery frozen shrimp because it was simpler to fix the same thing night after night. When company came, I made fish stew because it was impossible to screw up. No matter what you did to it, it tasted good. It was expandable, affordable, and good. On Friday night, my friends ate vats of it around my kitchen table.

Looking back, I can see that I arranged those evenings so that everyone but one man would go home. I liked living alone, but I didn't always want to go to bed alone. More and more often, a tall, blond intern from Cook County Hospital stayed behind, moving his possessions in bit by bit. First he got to keep his clothes and books on a chair, then he got his own peg in the closet. After he took possession of the bottom drawer of the dresser, we admitted we loved each other enough to let both our leases go and move into our own apartment. We got married a few months later.

Although it may be pointless to admit it, one of the benefits of those rootless years was the option of keeping a man—or anyone else, for that matter—at arm's length. When you live alone, there is a point when you can shut the door on the people and their quirks and indulge your own oddities as I did. While the intimacy of marriage is, quite simply, irreplaceable, to get it you must give up both privacy and control.

Only a woman going to bed when she is still angry with her husband understands how much territory the expression "consorting with the enemy" covers. She also understands the infinite time span of a phrase like "till death do you part." When you are married, you are stuck with the petty anger of it, the minor infractions, the forgotten domestic promises, the little messes, the irritating habits.

Looking over my shoulder, my old single life seems charmed. When I lived and worked alone, I created my own life. There were no compromises, no hours, no rules except the ones I set, no disappointments except those of my own making. I defined domesticity. I designed my life from the furniture up. I flourished in that freedom. I was my own child. I reinvented myself. I put my time to good use, which made it possible for me to sink my roots in the rich soil of marriage.

Still, as I look back through a fog of nostalgia, it is easy to downplay the dreary, miserable, dead-broke side of that life. The price I paid for breathing space was an occasional unbearable loneliness that drove me from the house to a bar called O'Rourke's, where I drank with the regulars until closing time. Freelance work paid abominably, working alone could be just as boring as working in an office, and I could only repot plants at three A.M. so many times.

I would be hard pressed, now, to do without the sustenance of family, the elemental delight in children. Now that I know the bone-deep sense of ease that comes from sleeping next to the same man for years on end, now that I have been loved by children who put no conditions or limits on their love, I could never willingly return to living alone. Yet there is still something about being alone when you want to be alone that frees the spirit just as domesticity tethers it.

II. Laurie Abraham

Sometimes I am embarrassed because I have never lived alone. After eighteen years with my parents, I moved into a dorm room with a woman who became one of my closest friends. From there, I went on to share apartments with other women friends, men friends, a man who was not my friend, my best friend and her boyfriend, my lover, my lover and his best friend, and for good measure, my lover's ex-stepmother. In all, I have lived with ten people in the last four years, which works out to 2.5 roommates a year. (At this rate, by the time I'm fifty I will be on my seventy-second roommate.)

Money, or lack of it, has compelled me to double up, triple up, and once, quadruple up. I did not have much choice when I was making $3.35 an hour as a magazine intern. A year and a half ago I started earning enough money to get my own place but when the time came to move I never considered going it alone. My best friend from college, Lisa, needed a roommate, and, well, why not get an apartment together? But in conversations with older women, I feel as if I have to make excuses for my persistent cohabitation. Laurie must have a dependency problem, I imagine them thinking.

The truth is, I believe that one-name mailboxes represent the pinnacle of independence. Although living alone is sometimes extolled to the point of absurdity, I believe it does instill self-confidence and a feeling of accomplishment. At the very least, I'd learn to pay my bills without someone else's prodding—or learn to suffer in the dark. And I know that the other reason I might want to live alone is not nearly so lofty. Roommates can drive me crazy: dinners for two turn into dinners for three, the pillowcase my mom gave me becomes a shoeshine rag, my front windows are outlined with strings of

lights shaped like red peppers and spotted lizards. My boyfriend is the only roommate I could confront about violations
of my silent code. Since I haven't felt comfortable challenging
anyone else, I've resorted to screaming into my pillow: why
the hell does she keep putting the wineglasses where the water
glasses are supposed to be?

Next fall, the conditions will be right for me to give single
living a try. Lisa is moving to Texas, and instead of searching
for a replacement, I'm going to find a one-bedroom apartment
or studio. Lisa, always the congenial sort, says living alone is
not worth squeezing into a studio. "When you live with somebody, you have rooms." But small sounds good to me, warm
and almost secret. And aesthetics aside, I do not have
enough furniture to fill a bigger apartment, or the time to
tend to it.

My friend, Glenn, has the kind of place that would suit me.
His bed fits into a small square cubicle, with enough room left
over for a standing reading lamp and little else. Wooden doors
painted the same eggshell color as his walls slide shut to block
the bed from the main room, where I would put my couch and
the antique chair I bought a year ago. Shooting off of the main
room like a tentacle is a narrow kitchen with more than enough
cupboard space for my few pans and dishes. This apartment
would be at its best in winter, when I could shut the windows
on the noisy street and sip hot tea.

III. Carroll Stoner

I was twenty-three years old when I lived alone in the sixties. I am proud that I did it. But when I first moved into my own apartment, with no roommates, no boyfriend (we didn't call them lovers then, even if they were), no parent's name on the lease, I remember my feelings: pride and fear in almost equal proportions, overlaid by a kind of shame that I was revealing how unwanted I was.

Yes, I was making a declaration of independence. But there was also that admission of something that even now I cannot quite face. A sense of having been rejected? Maybe. Of not being with others because of some personal eccentricity, some oddness? Yes. Just twenty minutes before the women's movement came along and changed everything for us, I could almost read the shock on others' faces when I told them I lived alone. I loved it. Sort of.

That's not the case at all today. Now women who get married right out of college are considered the odd ones, predestined for a conventional life, a bit unadventursome or timid. But then, I knew only one other woman who lived alone. She became a lifelong friend, and still shocks me by doing exactly what she wants to do, including making herself a millionaire. She still lives alone, though there is a husband in her past and two children off at school. When I first met her and she told me she lived without any roommates at all, I remember the thrill and shock I felt. What a great idea.

So when I inherited a rent-controlled apartment from married friends who moved on, I loved both the idea and the reality. My own empty refrigerator, my own tiny garden that was soon filled with weeds, reading all night and not explaining why, the apartment's West Side Manhattan location in a neighborhood where I heard more foreign languages in a day than I'd heard all my life in the Midwest—these were now details in my own, independent life as a woman.

Years later, sitting with a group of mostly married women, I am surprised to hear a majority of us reflect that our happiest domestic time—not the happiest time in our lives, but the time of greatest domestic contentment—was when we lived alone. How can that be? From the vantage point of the maelstrom that is family life, feeling responsible for everyone's well-being, is it nothing more than that the island of solitude in our pasts looks so carefree, so peaceful? So delicious. So distant. So temporary.

I lived alone for exactly four months, just long enough to splurge on stationery at Tiffany with my new address engraved along with my name. Then I eloped and gave up my name, made my stationery obsolete, and bequeathed my precious apartment to a friend. From that moment on, I have never been alone. Instead, I have learned to create solitude when I need it. There is a spot in front of the fireplace where I prop myself up on pillows and read. I turn up my music and can isolate myself for entire evenings. It is almost enough.

Choosing an Apartment

LAURIE ABRAHAM

"We want to rent it," I mumbled to my sandals.

"Great," our new landlord Jim responded. "I've got the papers right here."

Jim had come prepared. He handed me and my roomate-to-be, Lisa, separate copies of the lease, and we sat on the stagelike window seat to read them. The window seat was an appropriate spot on which to consummate the deal. It was the first thing Lisa and I had noticed when we saw the apartment. In fact, the gleaming wedge of wood running the length of the front wall probably explained why we were sitting there signing the lease. All I can remember from the two typed pages—the American Bar Association model for legally ignorant tenants, according to Jim—is that Lisa and I cannot open a school in our apartment. And I need written permission before I take pity on one of the abandoned cats who live at the Humane Society two blocks from my office. I also remember that Jim's four-year-old instilled in me my first doubts about our new apartment. The boy was pushing his toy cars across our window seat.

"What's that noise?" little Matthew asked as the ink dried on our lease.

"You know what it is, it's a truck," I told him.

A truck!

The truck sounded as though it were rumbling through my

spacious new living room—the one I had appreciated for its track lights, miniblinds, and hardwood floors in fairly good condition. The first time we saw the apartment, Lisa and I had not forgotten to include "noise" on our checklist of potential problems, but perhaps the traffic had been unusually light that day, or maybe Clark Street was blocked off for a parade. Today I imagined that we would become objects of wonder, like a family who refused to leave their clapboard farm home after an interstate sliced through the front yard. "How could anyone live there?" kids would ask their mothers, pointing to our storefront apartment from the back seat of the car.

But there was no turning back. This former beauty parlor four blocks from Wrigley Field now was my home. Not that I didn't cry over it. When we left, Jim was vowing to put white paint on the ugly brown paneling in the utility room (or breakfast room, as Lisa and I envisioned it). We headed for a comforting diner, where I ordered my usual, the Waitress Special. This was no time to try banana pancakes. Lisa opted for hash and scrambled eggs, which she drizzled with Tabasco sauce. "We really did it," she repeated several times. "Yep, we did," I said, pushing three new keys on my tarnished "I Love Chicago" key ring. After more new-apartment talk and three cups of coffee, Lisa decided to take another look at the place. I decided to go home—to my old home, that is, the one that would be mine for only a month more.

My composure broke on the way to the car, when I saw a glowing orange For Rent sign in the window of a blue-gray Victorian with violet trim. I cried because there were no trees on our new street, because our apartment was not a brownstone, because the silver radiators were rusty. Anybody who has seen the apartment I was leaving would be surprised to hear that such details bothered me. There is not a single tree on the street, although a twenty-foot plastic giraffe acquired by the photographers who lived below me peered in the back window. I cried thinking that maybe my new apartment was dangerous because it was on the ground floor—reasoning that hardly justified the tears because my old place was in a much rougher neighborhood. The building lock had been broken for at least a month, my friends were afraid to take the train there at night, and the brother of one of my co-workers had been shot to death three blocks east.

Signing the lease meant I either planned to pay rent for two apartments or, once and for all, move out of the loft my longtime boyfriend and I had shared. After months of "I've got to get out of this place," "Okay, then, leave," "No, I can't. I love you," "I love you, too," I was going. I had stood in the front room of my new apartment, which was as big as three living rooms put together, and wished that Paul and I were moving there. It was the kind of room he likes: open, white, washed by light from a line of large, square windows. We had tried but failed to create a space like this in a rotting loft, and now I had just rented it.

It was so big that Lisa and I giggled as we pushed open the front door. We wanted to dance, or do cartwheels. We had a perfect setting for winter parties where men wear dark turtle necks and loose tweed pants, guests get drunk on red wine, and good talk gives way to good dance around midnight. The only problem was that I probably could not invite Paul to these parties: we were separating to "see" other people. It would be just like me to ask him to every party I threw and then complain to my mother that men never asked me out. Nonetheless, I regretted that Paul would not be helping me decide where to put my first adult possession, perhaps every young woman's first significant piece of furniture: a couch. Every place Paul and I had shared required renovation, not decoration. Here, we could spend Saturdays reading, or finding the right place to hang a picture. Housecleaning would be a lark compared with the months and months of rehabbing I had been through.

Lisa and I decided to take the apartment while standing by a plot of back-yard mud that Jim said he planned to sod. It was our second appointment, and we tried our best to act like

savvy tenants. Lisa made sure the water rushed from the
bathroom faucet, and I opened and closed a few kitchen cabinets. Within minutes, we escaped out the back door to debate
the pros and cons of 3814 N. Clark Street. Pros: big front
room, window seat, free washer and dryer, freelance photo-
grapher/landlord with two kids, bars on the windows, six-foot
real wood fence in back. Cons: busy street, no trees, ugly
exterior, price.

Neither of us wanted to be the first to say "let's get it," and
as we debated I realized that I had never done this before. My
life's journey had been an up-to-date version of moving from
Daddy's house to husband's house. I had gone from Mommy's
house (my parents are divorced), to college dorm, to boyfriend's house. True, I had shared an apartment with friends
during college. And as a newspaper intern, I had spent three
miserable months in a dank efficiency in South Florida. I even
traveled alone in Europe one spring and summer. To an out-
sider, I probably seem fairly independent, yet someone else
had always decided where I would live.

Now that the responsibility is mine, I worry that I will not
be able to afford this new place, that I should have searched
harder, that when I am offered my dream job in New York I
will have to turn it down because I cannot break the lease. I
fear Lisa will plaster our walls with tattered peach posters, or
that I will come home in the middle of August to find white
twinkling lights draped across the windows. She fears I have a
latent love of the country look. Nevertheless, we are both
excited to move in. Our first party will be great.

Windows

The leather couches in my high-rise living room are honey-colored and down-filled, and to sit in them, even just to run a hand over them, is a sensual experience. The coffee table they enfold is a generous four feet across—large enough to accommodate a week's worth of newspapers and books and a jillion coffee cups. The view from floor-to-ceiling windows through which the sun pours on Sunday mornings is a midwestern version of "Sunday at la Grande Jatte": sun worshippers and cyclists and dog walkers and rugby players around a small lagoon in the midst of a dappled greensward, beyond which lies the lake where sailboats billow and bob. Who, one might think, could ask for anything more?

The only trouble is that since we moved here, most of my time seems to be spent sitting on the couch, drinking coffee, and looking out the windows. I'm exaggerating, of course. When he and I get home from the office we also shop, make dinner, pick up, do the laundry, play with our daughter, spend a little time at our at-home desks, and so forth. But still, when I think of our living room, I think mainly of sitting—and I don't like it.

I will acknowledge that the Calvinist work ethic runs rampant in this family. I mean, there are people out there who do not beat their breasts for moral laxity because they relax in the evening after a day's work. Nonetheless, there is something about our living room that encourages passivity, or perhaps it is constraint, and it seems to me that if I could discover what it is, I could change my life.

In the old house that preceded this one, the sofa was cloth-covered and made you sit up—unless you slid so far down that your neck hit the back. The coffee table was the size of a large dinner plate, which meant books and coffee cups rose in teetering piles about our feet. And although the country view was at least as splendid as this one (Brueghel instead of Seurat—round hills and haywagons and barnyard beasts), the windows seemed to look not out but in. While we certainly sat there of an evening, reading and drinking coffee, just as we do now, the feeling was entirely different. I felt contained rather than constrained; held, if not in the palm of a hand, certainly in a place that was protective, tolerant, and private.

Here in this apartment of many windows and a sweeping view, I feel somehow adrift, exposed, and, although it doesn't seem to follow, as idle as Coleridge's painted ship upon a painted sea.

At first I thought it was the luxury, which can be daunting when you're not used to it. But since the early days when I used to walk swiftly past the doorman with my head down so I didn't have to talk, the leather couches have accumulated a gray patina of cracks and the white carpeting a multitude of stains, so I have had to look elsewhere for the cause. It's occurred to me lately that it might be the windows.

My husband thinks I'm crazy. It is, he points out, a per-fectly beautiful apartment, and the windows through which the sun streams and through which life outside can so readily be observed are not the least of it. He hopes never to leave this place. I, too, love the sunshine streaming in, but something else—my spontaneity? my initiative?—seems to be slipping out. The signs are small and insignificant to anyone but me: a natural predilection for neatness rounding the bend into prissi-ness; a reluctance to start projects that make messes; a certain vagueness in my movements. I find myself standing here or

there, halfway across the room, an actor who has forgotten the
blocking, uncertain of where to go, what to do. The room feels
like a stage where I am a player—and the room doesn't feel
entirely real because of it.

Perhaps it's not the windows after all, but the absence of a
wall—actually, of two walls. Decorators and magazine people
have a term for it: "bleeding," meaning that the room or the
page tends to spill into empty space, to send its contents
sliding into the boundless universe. But I don't feel so much
that I am sliding out as that I am not entirely in.

I could live with pleasure in an all-glass house—if it were in
the center of a small sunlit clearing surrounded by a large
woods. Or I could live, as I did once, in a snug house of few
windows—if they looked out on an endless vista of field and
sky. It's all a matter of balance. We once moved from a house
because it had too many rooms we never used. All that empty
and foreign space made us feel ill at ease. Another time we
lived in an apartment that looked out upon a blind brick wall.
We wove a macramé lattice across the window and hung
plants from it, ostensibly to hide the ugly view, but today I
wonder if it wasn't that the yin/yang of window/wall was
offended by a window that looked out on a wall. What we are
talking about, it occurs to me, is neither windows nor walls
but a sense of enclosure.

How much enclosure anybody needs is a complicated matter and a personal one, depending on such things as the height
of the ceiling, the color of the walls, the closeness of the neighbors, the arrangement of the furniture, the aspects of the
weather, the geography of the terrain, and the state of the soul.
But there's no question in my mind that a sense of enclosure is
the essence of house, a matrix that we carry with us from
childhood, perhaps from before birth, and that resonates with
a Jungian echo through all the houses of our lives. For with
enclosure comes protection, and with protection, safety and
freedom: the freedom to be who you are, to do what you like,
to make a mess, to leave it be. The opposite of enclosure is, of

course, exposure, and that—even though it is southern—is what we have a little too much of around here. It just may be that even in a room with a view, the most important view you get is of yourself.

THE AUTHORS

When Laurie Abraham, twenty-six, began work on this book, she feared she had only one feeling about her home: Who needs it? But domestic life sneaked in through the back door: She has rehabbed a loft, hunted for an apartment with a roommate, learned to share a home, and learned to live alone. When her job as a public health reporter gets tough, Laurie fantasizes about pushing an umbrella stroller to the natural food store at eleven on a Wednesday morning.

Laura Green, forty-eight, is a journalist who has written about women and social change for a variety of publications. Formerly a newspaper reporter, magazine editor, and an assistant professor at Northwestern University's Medill School of Journalism, she recently moved to New York, where she is reinventing her home, her family, and her work. She has two children and a house on a hill.

Mary Beth Danielson, thirty-eight, the conscientious objector of the group, dropped out of the working world when her first child was born. She was briefly a minister in the United Methodist Church and has recently returned to school to get a graduate degree in English literature. Mary Beth believes that all women need to discover who they are and that some women will make this discovery at home. The mother of two young children, she is politically active in the sanctuary movement.

Nancy Eberle was the mother of three grown sons and a pre-teen daughter when she died in 1988. Nancy had been a newspaper reporter and vice-president of the Chicago Board Options Exchange. Her first book, *Return to Main Street*, chronicled her family's move to the country. After living on their farm for five years, she returned with her family to live in a city high-rise apartment.

Janice Rosenberg, forty-four, a traditionalist and self-professed perfectionist, has developed systems for domestic living that encompass everything from how to build bookshelves to how to raise children. She is a writer of both fiction and nonfiction, but her primary interest is in those elusive moments of grace that occur when you least expect them in family life. She is the mother of two.

Carroll Stoner, forty-seven, has launched a business career after a twenty-year career as a newspaper manager. In the past few years, she has made a fresh commitment to her family and promised to keep her domestic life in better balance with paid work. She originated the idea for *At Home* and writes about mastery within the home and things she wants her nine-year-old daughter to know. She is also the mother of a college-age son and two stepchildren. She and her family live in an apartment on a busy city street.